CRYPTOCURRE₁CY AND NFT INVESTING FOR TEENAGERS

HOW TO BECOME RICH IN YOUR TEENS BY
INVESTING IN BITCOIN, MEME COINS, ICOS,
NFTS (NON-FUNGIBLE TOKENS), AND BECOME
A SUCCESSFUL CRYPTO INFLUENCER

ALEXANDER KNIGHT

CONTENTS

CRYPTOCURRENCY AND NFT INVESTING FOR TEENAGERS

How to Become Rich in Your Teens by Investing in
Bitcoin, Meme Coins, ICOs, NFTs (Non-Fungible Tokens)
and Become
A Successful Crypto Influencer

Legal & Disclaimer

The information contained in this book and its contents is not designed to replace or take any form of medical or professional advice. It is not meant to replace the need for independent medical, financial, legal, or other professional advice or services, as may be required. The content and information in this book has been offered solely for educational and entertainment purposes only.

This book's content and information has been compiled from reliable sources, and it is accurate to the best of the Author's knowledge, information, and belief. However, the Author cannot guarantee its accuracy and validity and cannot be held liable for errors and omissions. Where appropriate and necessary, you must consult a professional (including but not limited to your doctor, attorney, financial advisor, or such other professional advisor) before using any of the suggested remedies, techniques, or information in this book. Further, changes are periodically made to this book as and when needed.

Author has not obligation to warrant the accuracy or appropriateness of any third-party websites or URLs. The listing of any person, business hyperlinks, or others in this book does not constitute an endorsement or recommendations by the author.

If a reader chooses to click on links and be taken to an external website belonging to a third party, then the reader and only the reader shall be responsible and liable for his/her actions should you suffer or incur any harm or loss from the usage of such information.

Upon using the contents and information contained in this book, you agree to hold harmless the Author from and against any damages, costs, and expenses, including any legal fees potentially resulting from the application of any of the information provided by this book. This disclaimer applies to any loss, damages, or injury caused by the use and application, whether directly or indirectly, of any advice or information presented, whether for breach of contract, tort, negligence, personal injury, criminal intent, or under any other cause of action.

You agree to accept all risks of using the information presented inside this book.

You agree that by continuing to read this book, where appropriate and/or necessary, you shall consult a professional (including but not limited to your doctor, attorney, or financial advisor, or such other advisor as needed) before using any of the suggested remedies, techniques, or information in this book.

INTRODUCTION

Right now, as you're reading this, you're giving yourself an advantage. Learning how to invest in cryptocurrency and learning about financial literacy skills is truly valuable. The knowledge in this book can change your financial horizon and expose you to numerous opportunities that otherwise wouldn't be enjoyed. It all begins here. Sit down, grab a snack, and read on.

Investing in all forms is a great way to make money and plant the seeds to a financially secure future. As a teenager, the skills and habits that you develop will last for life, and it's instrumental that you develop these skills and habits as soon as possible. I wrote this book because investing has always been a source of passion, not to mention enjoying the financial benefits. No matter your age, no matter the amount of money available to you, you can invest if you choose to, and I hope this guide will help you do just that and do it successfully.

Are there any differences or similarities between saving and investing?

It is right to say that you can earn additional cash if you save or invest your money. Yet, saving is quite different from investing, although many people use the two terms inter-changeably.

Saving occurs when you put your money in a low-risk vehicle like money market and savings accounts. Such accounts are generally safe, but the earning returns you get will be low; the returns you earn may not cover inflation.

You are investing when you actively deploy your wealth into high-risk businesses like cryptocurrency. Investment earnings are sometimes so big that they can turn you into an overnight millionaire.

High-risk investments take time to materialize, so you should start investing your saved money now if you want to get rich at 30.

A cryptocurrency is a form of digital money that is also known as virtual currency or cryptocurrency. That means no actual coins or bills exist; all is done online. You can send a cryptocurrency to someone over the Internet without using an intermediary such as a bank.

Cryptocurrency has finally become the name on the lips of millions of people from various parts of the world. In the past decade, a lot has changed about the view of people on Cryptocurrency. At the same time, the impact of this innovation has been felt across the globe.

Thanks to the high level of advancement in technology, the concept of cryptocurrency has continued to penetrate the economic and financial systems of the world.

Many people no longer view money as a commodity carried around in sacs and bags alone. They now have a rebranded view of money as a commodity that has been digitalized and can be transacted without the full influence of external factors such as unfavorable policies of financial institutions.

The history of cryptocurrency can easily be traced back to the early '90s when David Chaum created the first online money ever! The name of this cryptocurrency was known as Digicash.

Earlier in 1982, David Chaum had taken the bold step to stimulate people's attention about the birth of cryptocurrency when he released a paper titled: 'Blind Signature for Untraceable Payments.'

David Chaum sort to sensitize the general public about the new technological revolution known as Digicash which would serve as the first digital money with a solid secured system. This would allow transactions to be done outside the influence of the government or other external influences such as banks and similar financial institutions.

David Chaum released subsequent papers to highlight the modulus operandi of digital currency. One of his major works was centered around the assurance that double-spending will be prevented through offline transactions and other measures to ensure that the new technology having untraceable payment system does not have major loopholes that could discourage investors and users alike.

Exactly on the 27th of May, 1994, Digicash was released to symbolize the background works and activities of David Chaum and his team to create the 'World's first electronic cash payment over a computer network.'

Four years later, Digicash would go bankrupt and sold to e-cash technologies. The most logical reason for the failure and inability of Digicash to live to its promises was largely because most people at the time could not access the Internet. Nevertheless, David's works laid the base work for the likes of Bitcoin to sprout out later in the late 20's to fully present the potential of cryptocurrency.

As Digicash faded away and couldn't stand the test of time, the ideology of digital money wasn't going to fade with it. The likes of e-Gold came about to establish that transactions could be done over the Internet without physical interactions and influence. E-Gold thrived on the idea of receiving gold from registered users and in give the worth equivalent e-gold credit to them. This digital operation mode wanted to ensure that people needed not to carry their golds around before turning into 'untraceable' money that governments would have no influence over. However, owing to the fraudulent activities of certain people to exploit the deficiency of the e-gold system, the platform could not fully serve the return purpose of its existence.

Fast forward to 2009, a revolutionary technology known as the blockchain was born by the anonymous Satoshi Nakamoto. Blockchain is known widely in cryptocurrency as the decentralized system that allows individuals to transact digitally without government interference or other external forces. Blockchain technology transactions are safe with a robust system in place and can be traced throughout the blockchain system.

The anonymous Nakamoto created Bitcoin with blockchain, which has become the most popular and the most powerful amongst all cryptocurrencies ever created to date. Since 2009, Bitcoin has become more accepted and utilized by some individuals and institutions worldwide. Countries such as Japan and Canada have even gone ahead to place tax measures on transactions involving Bitcoin.

Due to the increasing value of Bitcoin overtime, more and more people have been looking at making money from Bitcoin and other cryptocurrencies.

In the subsequent chapters of this book, we shall discuss Blockchain technology, Cryptocurrencies, Bitcoin, and how to make money digitally with Bitcoin.

HOW TO EARN MONEY TO INVEST IN CRYPTOCURRENCY

'If you don't find a way to make money while you sleep, you will work until you die.'— Warren Buffett.

I know this is an investing book, but you can't invest unless you have the funds to invest in the first place; there's no way around it.

Many people think that you have to be an adult to make money, and most don't even start because of that. Others are too lazy, don't see the point, or are busy with other things.

Nevertheless, especially as a teenager, it makes sense and is feasible to earn money. I want to show you a couple of exciting methods to earn money as a teenager.

Where to find jobs?

Jobs or assignments can be found in different ways. One way would be to type in the job title + the city on Google. If you search for "babysitter jobs," you will find several sites where you can apply.

In addition, you can look around on many different job

portals and sites. These often even have a search filter where you can specifically search for jobs for teenagers.

There is also the possibility of finding advertisements in newspapers that suggest job offers. Even though the trend is moving towards digital job ads, it is still possible to find something here.

However, it doesn't always have to be the Internet or looking in newspapers. The old tried and tested method is still to ask around among friends and acquaintances. The probability of being hired is relatively high here. There is already a specific trust bonus here since they already know you.

Nowadays, there is also simply the possibility of looking in social media, quite simply via Facebook. Admittedly, many people claim that the whole thing doesn't make sense and that you should instead rely on the classic job portals. But I think that these people are still mentally living in the last century. After all, anyone who hasn't missed out on getting a smartphone knows that it's still feasible. You have to look around: There are quite a few groups on Facebook where hundreds of jobs are posted daily. You can type "jobs" in the search bar at the top, then filter by "groups," and here you go. You will get access to quite a few jobs.

Delivering newspapers

Let's start relatively simple with the first job. Almost everyone who has ever thought about earning money as a teenager sooner or later comes across the topic of delivering newspapers. That's why this topic simply had to be mentioned in the first place, for the sake of completeness.

The vital question at the beginning is whether it is worthwhile to deliver newspapers in the neighborhood at all? Does it make sense at all, or is it just a lot of legwork for little money?

Delivering newspapers is legitimate if you want to earn

some money quickly and easily. In this job, it is possible to listen to music on the side, and most of the time, the whole thing is done relatively quickly, especially if you are provided with a unique bicycle.

If the employer wants to pay you by the piece, though, I'd be a little wary. The hourly wage is often quite low if you are paid by every unit you deliver, especially if the houses have a large distance. That's why you should always look at this in advance.

In my opinion, this job is very suitable for teenagers and, like almost all things in life, has its advantages and disadvantages.

You are out and about in the fresh air and can organize your time flexibly.

One disadvantage, however, is the amount of walking. So if you don't like walking or cycling, then I'm sure there are plenty of alternatives you can do instead.

Babysitting

Another option is babysitting. Unlike many people, this job is not just about sitting next to the baby and waiting for time to pass. Babysitting usually involves additional tasks, such as caring, cooking/feeding the baby, preparing bottles, and even changing diapers if necessary.

Still, babysitting is the more flexible option compared to delivering newspapers because you don't have to walk as much and you're mostly indoors.

However, I would check out the family beforehand and then decide if I'm up for it. You can just talk to the people in this regard and then negotiate the hourly rates individually. Alternatively, there are many job portals on the Internet where you can sign up and look for babysitting jobs in your area.

Looking after pets

However, it doesn't always have to be taking care of children and babies. If you are an animal-loving, responsible person and at the same time still enjoy dealing with animals, then taking care of pets can also be an exciting job. Unfortunately, many dog and cat owners out there can't spare the time necessary to take care of their four-legged friends. If you can help out at this point, you are already a tremendous help to many pet owners and very much in demand.

Compared to delivering newspapers, this job is more difficult to get since it requires a lot of trust, similar to babysitting. But how do you get this job? After all, it is good to know the pet owners first. If this is the case with you, you can, of course, ask the owners directly and get this way to the side job.

But if you don't know anyone from your environment whom you can ask, you can also post a note on the bulletin board. Otherwise, there is also the option to find people on Facebook.

Tasks include walking the animals, replacing food bowls, pet care, and grooming when the owners are not around. You can also play with the animals to keep them entertained. Especially animal lovers will find a lot of fun in this job, which is crucial after all.

Helping older people

Now let's move on to a job that's a little less action-packed. It doesn't always have to be show life or delivering newspapers, because you can also earn extra money in care jobs.

When it comes to shopping or getting the household back in shape, many older people need support. Some simply want a little care or help with everyday things. Like-wise, tasks such as visits to the authorities, accompaniment at doctor's appointments, housekeeping, or maintaining contact with family members are very likely. This job can also involve talking to people and reading a story now and then, playing board games, etc.

If you can help here and also deal with older people, then this job can be pretty interesting.

Delivering food

Especially in the times of online commerce, delivery services are booming. If you're looking for a job as a delivery person, it can be financially rewarding. Often you don't even need a driver's license because there are enough companies that provide their employees with bicycles or e-bikes.

You will sometimes get tips when you deliver food, so the hourly wage can be significantly higher.

Start your own YouTube channel

Another method that can bring you a lot of money in the future is to start your own YouTube channel. You can also combine this activity with other jobs because YouTube only allows users to earn money if they have reached 1000 subscribers and 4000 hours of watch time.

Until you get these subscribers together, it can take a little while. However, as soon as you reach 1000 subscribers on YouTube and the channel has been approved for monetization, you will also start getting paid around the clock, as soon as someone sees the ads and clicks on them.

In addition, you can enter into paid partnerships with companies so that, depending on the number of subscribers, you can sometimes earn four-digit amounts.

Later, you can also sell merchandise, promote your own or other people's products, and stream on Twitch, for example, to get multiple sources of income.

Reselling

Fashion lovers have certainly heard of the term reselling. Many items are very hot right now and are traded at high prices. If you manage to buy them cheaply and sell them at a higher price, you can make significant profits.

Resellers usually buy Yeezys or Offwhite/Nike shoes cheaply on Instagram, Grailed, eBay, or StockX and then sell them higher.

Even though it might sound unrealistic at first, you can sometimes make more than 100 dollars profit per sale. If you sell 10 pieces per month and do it the right way, you can get to a turnover of 1000 $ and more.

Reselling is exciting, but it can also be very risky. It is recommended to always watch out for fake articles and other scams. Therefore, this job is not for everyone because you have to know the market very well, and you need a good feeling for distinguishing authentic/legit items and fake items.

If fashion is something you like, then reselling can be a fantastic idea. On Facebook, you can find many communities and groups, and there are many great books about this topic.

Mowing the lawn

Especially in the summer, some neighbors need help mowing the lawn. Often they simply don't have the time or don't feel like doing it themselves, so they hire someone to do it.

There is little you can do wrong when mowing your lawn. There is no special skill required, and depending on the size of the garden, it can be done relatively fast and easily.

But how do you find people who need help mowing the lawn? After all, there rarely are such ads in the newspaper.

One method, for example, could be to become active yourself and start looking out for people who need help. This can include simply asking around in the neighborhood and offering to help. You can also ask your parents or acquaintances if they know anyone who might be interested.

Alternatively, the whole thing also works very well via the Internet. Because you can simply get in touch with people there and place ads until you have the first 5-6 customers together. You can either do this for an hourly rate or offer it for 50 $, for example. Of course, this is always negotiable.

Dropshipping / E-Commerce

The world of online commerce! If you want to get a foothold here, dropshipping or e-commerce can also be the right way to start.

These methods involve selling your product(s) or the product(s) made by someone else, running ads, promoting it on the Internet, handling returns if necessary, running contests, and just about all the activities that go into running a successful online store.

If you want to develop a new product and have some start-up capital, you can ask some factories to help you. But this is a lot of work, a lot of risks, and not necessarily a guarantee that it will turn out to be successful.

Many companies are looking for partners who want to sell their manufactured goods online. On large retailer portals such as AliExpress or BigBuy, you can get in touch with these people and find a couple of products to sell.

Platforms to create your online store can be Shopify, WooCommerce, Wix, or payhip. However, the topic of e-commerce always requires some research. If you do it the right way, it can be very lucrative. There are many useful books and video tutorials on these topics if you are interested.

Selling on Amazon

Closely related to e-commerce is selling on Amazon. Surely you have already ordered something on the platform, and you certainly know how much is bought there every day. The advantage of Amazon is that you don't have to create or even program your store in advance.

Amazon gives you the platform, which is also already frequently visited, and you can then upload your products there within a couple of days. The goal is to place these products as high as possible in the search results and get good reviews. In this way, as many people as possible will see your products.

Amazon also takes care of order fulfillment. So, unlike some other online stores, you don't have to worry about logistics, packaging, and shipping, and all that stuff.

You can fully focus on the product, marketing, and customer support. However, this also requires startup capital, which is why many people don't even start.

There are many tutorials, guides, and guidelines for Amazon FBA on the Internet.

If you feel you're a skilled writer or want to make money as a publisher, you might want to look into Kindle publishing. There are thousands of people who make a lot of money with Kindle Publishing. If they can do it, you can too. What's great about Kindle Publishing is that you have complete control over what you write. You have the option of writing fiction or nonfiction, as well as short tales or whole novels. On the platform, some people even produce magazine-style articles. Kindle Publishing is a service that connects you with your target audience. It's the ideal platform for folks who want to self-publish their work.

Temporary job

Now, these were some exciting self-employed jobs that can boost your sales and earn good amounts of money. However, I also know that there is always a high risk. It's not always that easy, and I think there is no job where you can get rich overnight.

Many young people are looking for a temporary job,

which is a perfect way to go. Here you can usually make money even faster, and you have absolutely no risk.

Temp jobs have been around for a long time, will always be around, and there's always pretty much always a need for people. There are so many possibilities on what you can do.

For example, you could ask a bakery or a store nearby. Sometimes, they need temporary help. Depending on what kind of store it is, of course, the tasks differ. A wide variety of jobs can be done, and it's pretty hard to summarize how the tasks ultimately turn out. It always depends on what is needed in the company.

For example, in a bakery, this could be a job at the cash register, preparing the dough, the oven post, washing up, tidying up, or forming buns. However, in most cases, all tasks are thoroughly explained to you, and you are taught all the essential things.

2

UNDERSTANDING CRYPTOCURRENCIES

"An investment in knowledge pays the best interest." - Benjamin Franklin

I f you have some cash in your wallet, take it out. Look at it and study it closely. If it's a paper bill you're holding, you may want to feel it. It can be rough and a bit thicker than ordinary paper. Feel the texture and the ridges from the raised printing. If you have a coin, hold it up and look at its edge and rim. While you're at it, imagine what a cryptocurrency looks like. You'd probably have a hard time because cryptocurrencies are formless and faceless but not worthless. Unlike hard cash, they are intangible. This is the reason why a lot of people are not convinced about these new currencies.

From their inception, cryptocurrencies continue to dominate the global market. Thousands of people have already made millions of dollars from cryptocurrency investments, and they continue to do so. If you'd invested $500 way back in 2008, you would have become a multi-millionaire by now. This dramatic surge of profits and return on investment has encouraged some people to jump on the bandwagon. A lot have invested, and they're just sitting down now, watching their digits increase. They believe in the potential of cryptocurrencies, and so they leaped into the opportunity. However, to the average-income earner, cryptocurrencies can be incomprehensible. They're hard to fathom as they cannot be seen nor felt.

This chapter will define cryptocurrencies, study their distinguishing qualities, why they're getting popular, and whether they're legal. We will also tackle some types of cryptocurrencies and their worth.

Some Words to Crunch

There are words repeatedly used in this book. Familiarize yourself with them so you can easily follow the drift.

- Airdrops- This is the process of giving away cryptocurrency tokens for free
- Altcoins- These are alternative coins for bitcoins
- Bitcoins- These are digital or virtual money
- Blockchain- It is a sequence of blocks that are embedded with data
- Coin Burn- It is the permanent withdrawal of coins from circulation
- Cryptocurrency- Cryptocurrency is coined from "crypto," which means secret, and currency which means money. Putting these two words together, cryptocurrency means secret money
- Cryptography-This is the process of encrypting messages with codes
- Cryptocurrency Wallet- This is a software specially designed to accumulate cryptocurrencies
- Ethereum- This is another kind of cryptocurrency; it's next to bitcoins in terms of value
- Forking- It is the splitting of blockchains into two branches

- Hash Speed- The speed by which the cryptocurrency device works
- Nodes- Nodes refer to the computers that run the cryptocurrency blockchain
- Mining- This is the process of producing encrypted codes that link the blocks to the chain
- Smart Contract- This is an agreement in computer code entered between two or more individuals

What are Cryptocurrencies?

In this fast-changing world, cryptocurrencies are becoming a lucrative investment.

Cryptocurrencies are virtual money or currencies that employ cryptography in effecting and verifying a value transaction. Transactions are internet-based, so you need to have access to the Internet when you perform your exchanges.

Cryptography ensures the identity of users by obscuring the original text or data inputted in the blockchain by converting it into unintelligible codes. The encryption secures the information, and once recorded, it can no longer be modified.

There's a growing number of cryptocurrencies, but the most popular are Bitcoins and Ether.

Distinguishing Features of Cryptocurrencies

For you to understand more about cryptocurrency, here are some of its distinguishing features.

Liquidity

Liquidity is essential for all tradable assets. This means that assets and security can be easily converted into cash without disturbing the market price of such assets. Cryptocurrencies are pretty much like hard cash. You can use them to purchase almost anything like cars, home appliances, furniture, electronics, or food and drinks. Cryptocurrencies can also be turned into fiat currency if you prefer to make purchases and pay debts with physical money.

High liquidity is much preferred as this allows participants to trade easier. Low liquidity is disliked as this implies volatility of cryptocurrencies resulting in spikes of prices. How can you check the liquidity of cryptocurrencies? Just log in to any cryptocurrency exchange, check the order book that displays all buy orders and sell orders. The order book will give you an idea of the coin pair you're interested in and check whether it's liquid or not.

Decentralized

Decentralized cryptos are more popular. They're unique because they give their users control, plus there are no transaction fees. What does 'decentralized' mean?

The crypto dictionary defines this as a system not owned or controlled by a single entity, like a government, bank, or company (cryptoDefinitions, n.d.).

Unlike fiat currency, cryptocurrencies are decentralized, meaning no authorities or banks control the system. Transactions are processed and verified through a distributed and open network owned and controlled by no one.

Nodes are responsible for storing, preserving, and spreading blockchain data. Each node is called a peer. Interactions are made between peers, hence, the peer-to-peer (P2P) network. This system allows the transfer of currencies from anybody in any part of the globe for as long as there's the Internet and the subject can access another's crypto wallet. All of these can be done without any intervention by any bank or by the government.

Anonymous

Transactions involving cryptocurrencies occur in an encrypted channel via cryptographs. However, with bitcoins, transactions are only partially anonymous or pseudo-anonymous for the very reason that the IP address of the user can be traced through network analysis. Other cryptocurrencies such as Zcash and Monero have greater anonymity, making the transactions secure and private.

Anonymity is based on the trust given to the people or the organization you are dealing with. Are there ways to ensure the anonymity of the blockchain?

Fortunately, yes. There are some measures to maintain the anonymity of the blockchain through a set of practices such as using Tor, VPNs, unique crypto addresses for new transactions, and ironclad wallets.

Security

Just how secure are blockchains?

Since encrypted codes secure cryptocurrencies, they're hard to break. The numbers used in the encryption are so huge, it's almost impossible to crack them. Also, an owner has a private key. Nobody else can access this private key except the user. Unless, of course, the users share the private key with someone else.

Blockchain enables confidentiality via a "public key infrastructure," which is a tool for encryption. This protects the blockchain against any malicious attempts to alter data. The size of a ledger has to be large and well distributed so that the network will be more secure.

Irreversibility

So, is the block irreversible? To some degree, yes.

Transactions cannot be canceled or altered once they're recorded on the blockchain. Cryptography makes this almost impossible as you need to change every node in the blockchain. So, before you confirm any transaction, check it twice or thrice. Once entered, the data cannot be undone anymore, and it will just remain in the blockchain.

Is irreversibility a good thing? In some ways, yes. It's good for merchants because it reduces any chance of getting defrauded. It also reduces conflicts arising from transactions. It's also suitable for users since they don't need to pay any processing fees.

Why are cryptocurrencies so popular?

There are numerous reasons why cryptocurrency has become the talk of the town. Aside from the distinguishing features already discussed. You can explore these three main reasons: cheap, no ties with any government, and the promise of Profit.

Cheaper Transaction

Processing fees such as exchange fees, wallet fees, and network fees are kept to a minimum. This is one of the reasons why a lot of people prefer cryptocurrencies. Tron and Bitcoin Cash collect fees that are lower than one percent of the value of these currencies, thus offering a win-win deal.

No Ties to the Government

The no-strings-attached characteristic of cryptocurrencies sustains their stability. Since no ties with any government, investors are lured into investing and protecting their wealth through cryptocurrencies. Third parties like banks or other financial institutions are eliminated from the picture. You can set aside any fears that your crypto assets will be seized by any public authorities or even the developers of those cryptocurrencies themselves. You can keep your funds knowing that they are safe if you safeguard your private keys.

The promise of Profit!

There is a potential for a considerable return of investment in dealing with cryptocurrencies. This can be done through various modes: staking, buying, holding, trading, referring, and getting some bonus or tokens. With proper education and a degree of hindsight, cryptocurrencies can indeed offer a lucrative opportunity to increase your financial assets.

How do Cryptocurrencies Work?

To explain the mechanism of how cryptocurrencies work, let's break down the steps into three stages: initiating a transaction, blockchain at work, and mining.

Initiating the Transaction

Transactions are performed through a P2P network by using cryptocurrency wallets. The person initiating the transfer of funds opens his account by typing in the private key. Before confirming the transaction, all inputs must be checked since actions can no longer be reversed once they're encrypted and recorded in the public ledger.

Blockchain at Work

When you look at it, cryptocurrencies work much like debit cards. The difference lies in who issues the currencies and keeps the ledgers. Instead of banks, it's the complex system of algorithms that does all the work. The good thing with crypto is that you don't deal directly with someone else. You don't need to go to the bank and wait for clearance. So, what does all the processing and storage of data do?

Meet blockchain.

Blockchain records information about the sender, the recipient, the amount of cryptocurrency, and the time. All these will be encrypted. Transaction amounts are made public; however, the sender's identity remains hidden.

Mining

Once the transaction is recorded and encrypted in the blockchain. Miners will try to find solutions to the cryptographic puzzle using high-performance computers. The task is done through a process called mining. The first miner to decipher the codes will be earning small amounts of cryptocurrencies. Once this is over, the transaction gets validated, and the block is added to the blockchain.

Is mining cryptocurrencies a profitable activity? Yes, in

the earlier inception of bitcoins. The first bitcoin ever mined cost 50 BTC, which is equivalent to 6,000 USD at that time.

So, how do you become a Bitcoin miner? First, create a bitcoin wallet, then join a mining pool, a group of miners who combine their resources and hashing schemes to mine more bitcoins. Their pooled profits will be evenly distributed to each member.

3

BITCOIN AND BLOCKCHAIN

"Blockchain technology could change our world more than people imagine." – Jack Ma

There are many misconceptions about bitcoins and blockchains. Some even interchange these words, and others think that they're the same as cryptocurrency. To set the record straight, bitcoin is a type of cryptocurrency. Bitcoins are processed and stored in a digital platform called a blockchain. In other words, bitcoins are inside the blockchain.

You'd probably ask if there's only one blockchain or public or private, whether it's being controlled by a single person or by a group of individuals. You may also wonder how bitcoins are minted and exchanged. You may want to know whether the file storage of blockchain operates like a cloud where you can store documents and other files. You'll have the answers in this chapter.

This chapter will help you deepen your knowledge more on bitcoins and blockchains. The discussions are presented in an easy-reading and straightforward method. So, are you ready?

We'll start with bitcoin. Bitcoin is the root of all this craze about cryptocurrencies. When it was introduced in 2008, it was muted. Some were skeptical and reserved about it, but some got curious. Who could have known then that bitcoins would become so phenomenal?

Everything You Need to Know About Bitcoins

Over the years, the use of bitcoins has grown tremendously as more people are getting hooked on bitcoin investments. The fears and doubts about bitcoins are slowly fading as people begin to see the results of these cryptocurrencies.

A bitcoin is a digital currency transferred from person to person using computers, gadgets like smartphones, and the Internet. It is by far the most common and highly valued type of crypto. Once you have stashed some bitcoins in your crypto wallet, you can't see them since they're in the form of electronic currency. You can't hold them, but you can be assured that they're safely tucked in cyberspace.

The Man Behind Bitcoin: Satoshi Nakomoto

It was on August 18, 2008, when the domain bitcoin.org was listed on the Internet. In the same year, Satoshi Nakomoto, an unknown person, or group of persons, published the bitcoin whitepaper, *Bitcoin: A Peer-to-Peer Electronic Cash System*. There were mixed reactions. Some were curious. Some didn't agree with it.

After the publication of the bitcoin whitepaper, the software debuted to a bit of fanfare in 2009. From then on, anybody can download and access the software.

In May 2010, the first-ever bitcoin purchase was recorded. These were two pizzas from Papa John's bought at 10,000 BTC. The bitcoin community started to grow. Satoshi stayed on for a while to work on the codes and make some patches. Then he surrendered all control of the bitcoin website to Gavin Andresen, one of bitcoin's earliest developers. No one has heard from him since.

There are many speculations about the identity of Satoshi Nakomoto. Nobody knows who they are, whether they are an individual or a group of people. They kept his identity well hidden. Up to this day, the search for the real Satoshi continues. Some claimed that he is Hal Finney, a cryptographer who helped in the early development of bitcoin. There are similarities between his style of writing and that of Satoshi. Others believe that Satoshi is Dorian Nakomoto, the neighbor of Hal Finney. Dorian Nakomoto denied any connections with bitcoin. Still, many thought that Satoshi and Dorian are the same though this was never confirmed.

It seems that Satoshi's real identity will never be revealed. He disappeared from the limelight, but his bitcoins continue to rule the global market. After all, he deserves some commendations both for his efforts in creating bitcoin and for staying anonymous for almost 13 years. Let's admit it! Satoshi's P2P payment system is extraordinary, and it enacted revolutionary changes in how people make payments without a mediator.

Characteristics of Bitcoins

Just like other cryptocurrencies, bitcoins are decentralized. This means that they're not within reach of the government, banks, or any individuals. The users enjoy freedom in dealing with bitcoins. Inflation is out of the question since there can be no surplus in the production and printing of currencies. The number of bitcoins produced is limited; hence bitcoins are scarce.

Purchases made by using bitcoins aren't taxable. This is one advantage. You'll pay for the goods without having to worry about Value-Added Tax (VAT). Transactions are pretty fast, like any other cryptocurrency. Anonymity is also guaranteed if you safeguard your password or private key.

Drawbacks of Bitcoins

You might want to ask if there are negative things about bitcoins. As a matter of fact, yes. There are some downsides that you need to be aware of.

- Once you lose or you forget your private key, you lose all your bitcoins. You've got to safeguard that password lest you want it falling into the hands of people who are going to rob you off with your digital reserves

- You cannot transact without the Internet. Since bitcoin transactions are Internet-based, you've got to connect to the World Wide Web. There's no offline transactions. Everything has to be done via the Internet

- Early adopters of bitcoins gain more. Those who started investing in Bitcoins earlier are getting richer as the value of bitcoins increases over the years

- Bitcoins can be replaced with better cryptocurrencies. Since there are other cryptocurrencies being continually developed, there's a chance that a better and stronger cryptocurrency can supersede bitcoins

- Governments have the power to ban bitcoins as they see fit. This is especially true when governments become suspicious of transactions, especially with the possibility of cyber-crimes lurking within the blockchain network

- The value of bitcoins is volatile. Bitcoins have experienced price fluctuations, and this puts a lot of investors on their toes

Forks in Bitcoins

Forking is how a blockchain splits into two chains, each having its own unique protocols. This is done whenever the blockchain is updated. Almost all divergences are considered a fork. Forks come in two forms: soft fork and hard fork.

A soft fork is an updated chain compatible with previous models or versions or simply termed backward compatible. Let's say you have an upgrade in your computer's operating system, and you have to open a file saved in an older version of Powerpoint, like Powerpoint 2016, and you will use the recent version of Powerpoint 2019. You can open the file because Powerpoint 2019 is backward-compatible.

A hard fork, on the other hand, is not interoperable with an older version or system. Once you use a hard fork, many nodes are needed to update the blockchain into a new version. Nodes updated get to use the new coins and blockchain, while the nodes that are not updated cannot access the new blockchain.

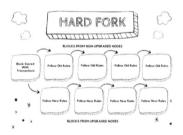

When do Forks Occur?

Forks occur when developers make upgrades on the blockchain due to attacks. There can be some substantial effect on the cryptocurrency forks, like a large price fluctuation. During the forking process, new currencies that look like bitcoin are created. Since 2009, there are already 105 bitcoin hard forks, but only 75 are active projects.

Segwit is a good example of a bitcoin soft fork intended to create two compatible versions of the blockchain that share one single asset, the bitcoin crypto.

Bitcoin Cash is an example of a bitcoin hard fork intended to make two different assets with value. After the forking, there are now two different cryptocurrencies: bitcoin cash and bitcoin.

What are the Effects of a Fork?

• One blockchain becomes more dominant than the other. One blockchain could be a better version than the other forked bitcoin

• One blockchain will be favored. Since one has better features, chances are it would be favored more

• Both blockchains co-exist, and if they stay active, there's a chance that each will fork at some point too

Bitcoin Versions

Here are some versions of bitcoins.

• Bitcoin XT- This was released in 2014. Its significant features are its higher transaction rate (from 7 seconds to 24 seconds), increased block size (from 1MB to 8 MB), and its ability to double its block size every 2 years

• Bitcoin Classic- This was released in 2016. Its significant features are: increased block size from 1 MB to 2 MB and doubled the transaction rate of the original bitcoin

• Bitcoin Unlimited- This was released to address the issue of the block size of bitcoin. Instead of giving the block size from the start, users are allowed to decide on the block size themselves

• Bitcoin Cash- This was released in 2017. It is by far the most successful hard fork of bitcoin. Its notable features are block size of 8 MB; the proof-of-work is easy to adjust, and no Segwit feature

• Bitcoin Gold- This is a hard fork of the original open-source cryptocurrency

TYPES OF BLOCKCHAIN

There are four major types of blockchains. These are: private, public, hybrid, and federated.

- Public Blockchain- This type of blockchain is decentralized, with nobody controlling the network. Data is secure and unalterable once a block has been validated and added to the blockchain. Almost anybody can join in the transactions. An example of a public blockchain is bitcoin and Ethereum

- Private Blockchain- This is a permissioned blockchain. Only a few selected and verified participants can join the network. Users need to get permission before getting access to the network from the person-in-charge in managing the blockchain. A good example is Hyperledger Fabric

- Hybrid Blockchain- This type of blockchain uses the combined qualities of public and private blockchains. It provides controlled access, but the users still enjoy freedom. The structure of this type can be customized

- Federated or Consortium Blockchain- Multiple organizations who use the network create a decentralized system. The Enterprise Ethereum Alliance (ESA) is an example of federated blockchain.

The Structure of Blockchain

Three main parts comprise a blockchain.

- The Block- This is a list of information documented in a ledger. The list accumulates over time. The size of a block differs from blockchain to blockchain. Even the period and triggering event may vary. The block is the account book that contains all transactions made using your bitcoins, such as your purchases or remittances. A block contains a certain data, the hash of the block, and the hash of the previous block

- The data stored in each varies depending on the type of blockchain used. In the bitcoin blockchain, the block stores approximately 500 transactions with information on the sender, receiver, and number of coins

• The Chain- They call this the hash. It connects or links one block to another block. This concept is probably the hardest to explain as the whole mechanism is complex, and it's usually the cryptographs who understand them. In her book Blockchain for Dummies, Tiana Laurence described the hash as a fingerprint of data recorded, and the hash locks the blocks in order and time (Laurence, 2017). The hash also detects any changes in the block

• The Network- This is composed of nodes. These nodes are the users or computers within the blockchain. There are specific nodes called the miners responsible for verifying transactions before adding them to the blockchain structure. These nodes ensure the validity, security, and availability of data to authorized parties.

How the Blockchain Works

The blockchain makes all transactions possible. How does it work? There are seven steps:

1. A transaction is initiated
2. A block is formed
3. The block is transmitted to the nodes
4. The nodes validate the data
5. The nodes get rewarded for the transaction
6. The block is added to the blockchain
7. The transaction is completed

Whenever a transaction is initiated, a new block is created. Suppose Brad places an order for an eBook with Mary, and he sends the payment via the blockchain. He'll send the amount with a short message, "Payment for eBook." The message will be recorded and encrypted using a hash function that makes it impossible to crack down the codes. The data will then be shared through a P2P network all over the world.

Nodes within the blockchain execute algorithms to validate the transaction. If most of the nodes have authenticated it, the new block is then accepted into the ledger. If, however, a consensus is not met, the block is denied. A block is verified through miners. Miners will run a PoW in solving the encrypted message. If the block has been validated and accepted in the ledger, a miner receives a reward from the newly created cryptocurrency. The recipient will also receive the amount that the user has sent.

The Power of Blockchain

So, what's the whole point about a blockchain? What does it do exactly?

- It's accessed without the control of an authority
- It's used to create or transfer assets
- It's used to record transfers
- It's used to allow owners of assets to exercise their rights over ownership and to record such exercise of rights

Where Does Blockchain Use Cryptography?

Cryptography can be used in three primary stages:

- For initiating and publishing transactions using digital signatures and private keys
- For validation of transactions using PoW and other consensus algorithms
- For chaining blocks using hash functions

The Blockchain Ecosystem

Blockchains create a virtual community. There's an entire group of people interacting with one another. This whole blockchain economy consists of users, investors, miners, and developers. These groups are dependent on one another.

- Users- These are the common people who use cryptocurrencies for personal consumption, like buying and selling commodities and services. They may even venture into micro-investing by buying and holding cryptocurrencies

• Investors- This group forms part of a big chunk of the blockchain ecosystem. They believe in the investment capacity of the blockchain. They constantly look for the small-or large-scale investment they can make for possible expansion of their crypto assets

• Miners- They play a crucial role since they are the ones who validate every transaction that takes place. There's high competition here, as miners compete in decrypting the codes of every transaction. For every validated transaction, the miners are rewarded with the new cryptocurrencies created

• Developers- This is the group of people, programmers and developers who make applications and write programs. They work toward constantly improving blockchain technology for better performance and efficiency

To what group do you intend to belong? The users, investors, miners, or developers? Whichever you pick, you'd be a valuable addition to the entire blockchain community.

4

HOW TO BUY AND INVEST IN BITCOIN IF UNDER 18

"Do not be embarrassed by your failures, learn from them and start again." - Richard Branson

There are several ways that someone can get Bitcoin if under 18, but the most common are:

- By exchanging fiat currency for Bitcoin through an exchange
- Getting Bitcoin from someone else who already has Bitcoin
- Bitcoin mining

We will look at all of these methods, but before we dive in, we should look back at a more fundamental question: *Where do Bitcoins come from?*

Where Do Bitcoins Come From?

Who "makes" bitcoins? This is an important question, and it is related to another issue that you may be wondering about: how is the *value* of bitcoin determined?

To answer both of these questions, it is helpful to look briefly at where traditional fiat currency comes from. Governments and institutions control the printing of paper money. The amount of money that is printed impacts the value of that currency in the global financial market. The economics behind how this all works can get pretty complicated, but in a nutshell: the more money the government prints, the less *value* that currency generally has. In economic terms, this principle is often referred to as "scarcity," meaning that the less there is of something and the more people who want it, the more value it has. This concept applies to commodities, fiat currencies, and Bitcoin.

Throughout history, there are many examples of situations where a government has printed tons of paper money to cover short-term expenses (almost always related to war). As a result, the value of that currency has plummeted. The most well-known example of this is the hyperinflation in Germany's Weimer Republic after World War I. People famously wallpapered their houses with paper money because it had so little value.

One significant way that Bitcoin is different from fiat currency is that there is a hard cap on the number of Bitcoins created. No more than 21 million Bitcoins will ever exist. The last Bitcoin is estimated to appear sometime around the year 2140. This built-in scarcity is one crucial aspect of how the value of Bitcoin is determined.

Still, however, we have not answered the question of where Bitcoins come from. The short answer is that they are "mined" by Bitcoin miners.

Bitcoin Mining

If Bitcoins come from mining, it might be quite tempting to conclude that one should drop everything and become a Bitcoin miner. One of the first things that newcomers to the Bitcoin space often hear about is mining. At a glance, this can look like a primrose path to "free money." It can sound like mining is as easy as firing up an application on your laptop and watching the Bitcoins come rolling in! Unfortunately, like most things involving "free money," the reality is that mining is not so simple.

Earlier, we looked at the blockchain and how transactions are stored throughout a distributed network of computers. We know that each transaction is verified and added to the blockchain, but how exactly does this happen?

This is where miners come in. Bitcoin miners use special software to solve complex math problems used to verify transactions, maintain the blockchain and add blocks. By checking a new transaction against the public ledger of previous transactions (the blockchain), a "node" (a particular mining station) can distinguish between a valid transaction and an invalid one.

If someone attempts to spend Bitcoins that don't exist, the system will say, "Hey, wait a minute, this doesn't match up with the history on the blockchain..." and the transaction will be rejected. Miners handle the heavy-duty computer processing to check all new Bitcoin transactions, verify them, and add them to the blockchain.

In exchange for solving blocks, miners are rewarded with a certain amount of new Bitcoin, thus adding a little bit at a time to the global volume of available Bitcoins in circulation. This incentive encourages more people to mine, leading to a more secure system through wider distribution.

In the early days of Bitcoin, mining was something that could be done on pretty much any old computer and the reward for "discovering" a block was ample. At the same time, the overall value of Bitcoin was extremely low and there were not that many Bitcoins in circulation. Over time, as more and more people began to use Bitcoin and become miners, the conditions changed.

Built into the protocol behind Bitcoin is a relationship between the number of miners and the level of difficulty involved in solving the problem, or "mining" each block. In theory, we can imagine that if more miners enter the scene, more blocks will be created at a faster pace. The Bitcoin protocol works in such a way that as more blocks are created, the rate of difficulty involved in solving the complex math problems required to successfully "mine" a block goes up. By making it harder to mine a block, the rate of block creation goes down. This relationship between the number of Bitcoins and the difficulty involved in mining new ones keeps the ecosystem stable over time.

The level of difficulty, today, required to mine a block is so resource-heavy, both in computer power and electricity, that it requires special equipment. In most cases, the cost of a mining operation far outweighs what one could hope to earn from mining Bitcoin for a very long time. Today, many miners operate in collectives known as "pools," where members combine resources and split rewards. Joining a mining pool is one way to increase the odds of recouping the costs of mining equipment and potentially making a profit. It is still possible to earn Bitcoin today through mining, but it is not easy or free to get started.

Buying Bitcoin

While there is still opportunity in mining, it is not the most straightforward way to get your hands on some Bitcoin. It is much faster and easier to get existing Bitcoin from somewhere else than trying to mine new Bitcoin.

When it comes to acquiring Bitcoin in this way, you have several options. You will need to set up a Bitcoin wallet to receive and store your funds no matter which route you take.

Bitcoin Exchanges

In many countries, the easiest way to buy Bitcoin with

fiat currency is through an online exchange. Bitcoin exchanges work essentially like any other currency exchange, where you use one currency to buy another. In this writing, Coinbase is one of the most popular (coinbase.com) Bitcoin exchanges in the US. Coinbase is an online platform that creates a Bitcoin wallet for you, lets you connect your bank account, and buy or sell Bitcoin through a straightforward user interface.

Most Bitcoin exchanges involve transaction fees, and Coinbase is no exception. While it is technically "free" to use most Bitcoin exchanges, there will be percentage fees associated with most or all transactions. It is also not uncommon to experience delays when transacting through exchanges, ranging from mildly inconvenient to debilitating. Becoming familiar with the process and factoring fees and delay times into your transactions will make things run smoothly.

Most exchanges that allow you to buy Bitcoin with fiat currency will require you to link to a bank account and enter personal information. This allows for fast, convenient movement between fiat currency and Bitcoin. Once again, it will be worth it to do some research and be sure to use an exchange that can demonstrate some longevity and has a good reputation.

Even then, it is generally not a good idea to store all or most of your Bitcoin in an online exchange. Mt. Gox, famously, was the world's dominant Bitcoin exchange for several years. At the height of its popularity, Mt. Gox handled around 70% of the world's total Bitcoin transactions. Then, in 2014, there was a massive security breach and approximately 850,000 Bitcoins were lost or stolen under somewhat mysterious circumstances. Exchanges are helpful in moving funds between Bitcoin and fiat, trading, and actively transacting with Bitcoin. Still, the Mt. Gox fiasco is a good example of why it is not the best idea to keep all of your assets stored in an online exchange.

Bitcoin ATMS

Another way to buy Bitcoin that is becoming increasingly popular is through Bitcoin ATMs. These devices are cropping up all over the place, from malls to airports to city centers. They look a lot like traditional ATM's, but there are some important differences. Primarily, Bitcoin ATM's don't connect to any banks. They are connected, through the Internet, only to the universe of the Bitcoin network. Many Bitcoin ATM's allow for bidirectional exchange, meaning that you can either insert cash to be converted to Bitcoin and transferred to a public key address, or you can have Bitcoins from your account converted into cash and dispensed by the machine. Some only handle transfers one way or the other.

ATM's can provide a more anonymous way to buy into Bitcoin without syncing your bank account to a platform like Coinbase. However, depending on the machine, there may be high transaction fees and limits on how much you can deposit or withdraw. You can search for Bitcoin ATM's in your area by using the Coin ATM Radar website at https://coinatmradar.com/.

Getting Bitcoin From Someone Else

Since the beginning of Bitcoin, one of the most common ways to get started the currency has been finding someone willing to gift or sell some to you. As Bitcoin is a digital asset, it should not be too surprising that much of the Bitcoin community exists online. Forums such as bitcointalk.org or Reddit's r/bitcoin are good places to engage with other Bitcoin users. Some Bitcoin enthusiasts are happy to donate a small amount to a newcomer to help them establish their first wallet. After all, the more people that use Bitcoin, the higher the demand, thus the more valuable it will become, at least in theory. It makes sense from a long-term financial perspective to help new users get started through that lens, even if it means initially spending a little of your own coin.

There are also various online tools to find local Bitcoin exchanges, where people meet up offline, in person, to trade with Bitcoin. This can be a great way to avoid transaction fees, meet fellow Bitcoin enthusiasts in your area, and potentially increase the level of transaction anonymity. As with any scenario that involves meeting someone "from the Internet," use your judgment if meeting up to exchange Bitcoin locally.

Investing in Bitcoin

Particularly as Bitcoin has become more popular, there is a lot of advice floating around on making money with Bitcoin and other cryptocurrencies. In reality, there is no secret, easy, foolproof method to invest $100 and come out with $10,000. As with any market, Bitcoin trading is a risk and reward system, and there are no guarantees. Just because Bitcoin is a digital currency does not mean you can't lose "real money." Of course, you can *make* real money, too, but it is essential to remember that this is a high-risk space.

Compared to traditional markets, the cryptocurrency space is extremely volatile. Prices can fluctuate significantly over one day or even one hour. It is not uncommon to see values swing up or down by 20% or more in 24 hours. Particularly for traders coming from traditional markets, the peaks and crashes in the cryptocurrency space can certainly get your adrenalin pumping.

Many people have made the mistake of hearing about Bitcoin (or another cryptocurrency) for the first time, usually due to some hype, and immediately buying in while the price is high, thinking they will get in before it goes up even more. Then they see the price of the currency plummet. In a panic, they sell it all off to cut their losses before it sinks anymore, only to see it level out or soar a few days (or hours) again later. There is no way to guarantee that this will not happen even to savvy traders, but you can do a lot to improve your odds of success.

The single most important thing you can do as an investor in the cryptocurrency world is to do your own research. Arm yourself with good resources and take the time to study the trends. Particularly as Bitcoin has entered the mainstream, there has been a huge rise in self-proclaimed Bitcoin gurus, some of whom are more credible than others. Explore freely, but keep in mind that anything promising "instant wealth" is worthy of healthy skepticism.

A great way to get familiar with the landscape of Bitcoin exchanges is to spend some time looking at the charts. Study the peaks and dips, level of stability, and researching any anomalies. Did something happen at a certain point to trigger a huge jump or drop? Was there a significant global event, did an article come out in a popular magazine, did an industry leader begin accepting Bitcoin? Could a similar thing happen again? These are good questions to consider. Almost all Bitcoin exchanges have charts that graph the historical trends and offer real-time updates on value, volume, and other statistics. Coinmarketcap.com is one popular website that offers daily overviews, history, and information on a wide variety of cryptocurrencies.

The more information you have, the better equipped you will be to see new opportunities and avoid common mistakes. Get to know the Bitcoin space, read articles, engage with the community, and explore available tools and resources. Nobody can predict the future, but the more aware you are of trends on a moment-to-moment basis, the more likely you are to anticipate the behavior of the markets correctly. What you ultimately choose to do with your money is your business, but one famous adage that you may want to keep in mind is: *"Don't invest more than you can afford to lose."*

Bitcoin Exchanges and Trading

When it comes to "trading with Bitcoin," there are several ways that this can happen. The most basic way to do it is to buy Bitcoin with fiat (US dollars, Euros, etc.), wait for the price of Bitcoin to go up, and then exchange it back into fiat. Of course, there is no guarantee that the price will go up; it could just as easily go down. Being familiar with the trends, history, and current affairs can help you make informed decisions about when to buy in and cash out.

Some firm believers in Bitcoin might argue that this approach of trading between Bitcoin and fiat "misses the point." On an ideological level, there are valid reasons for that sentiment. Realistically, however, many people see Bitcoin as an investment and not a "replacement" for fiat currency. Whatever your opinion on the matter, the fact remains that people have increased their wealth by using this approach.

You can find a list of online exchanges that deal with trading between Bitcoin and national fiat currencies at https://bitcoin.org. To do this type of trading successfully, you will also want to be very conscious of transaction fees, delay times, and exchange reputability. These factors can all differ between exchange platforms and can change in response to any number of events or circumstances. All exchanges come with their own unique pros and cons. Accessibility to certain exchanges may depend on your nation of residence.

Some of the most popular exchanges in the US are Poloniex, Bittrex, GDAX, Coinbase, and Kraken. Once again, all of these have different features and may be more suited to a particular set of needs. Coinbase is widely considered to be one of the easiest platforms for beginners, as it allows you to buy Bitcoin with a large variety of national fiat currencies through a very user-friendly interface.

Bitcoin exchanges, in general, have an initial learning curve for many people, particularly those who are new to markets and trading. Even those coming from a background in the stock market may find that Bitcoin exchanges take some getting used to. All exchanges tend to have different rules, spending limits, levels of verification, security practices, and tools available. Plus, not all exchanges deal in all cryptocurrencies. Generally, however, all exchanges do trade primarily in Bitcoin.

"The Fast Nickel or The Slow Dime"

You may have heard an expression before about investing: *the fast nickel or the slow dime.* Essentially, this means making a little bit of profit in the short term or a larger profit over the long term. When it comes to trading Bitcoin, there are plenty of people who employ both of these strategies.

Some investors choose to buy Bitcoin once, ideally when it the value is low, and hold on to it, believing that the price will trend upwards over time and eventually pay off big-time. This worked out very well for early adopters who held on to their initial Bitcoin investments. Some speculate that Bitcoin will undergo another massive price increase in the future. These folks will continue to hold tight to their Bitcoin throughout price fluctuations, hedging their bets on long-term growth. This would be the "slow dime" approach. (Buying into a cryptocurrency and holding on to it is often called/spelled "hodling" in online cryptocurrency communities).

Others watch the space diligently and regularly shift funds back and forth between Bitcoin, fiat, and other cryptocurrencies, taking advantage of minor price fluctuations, somewhat similar to Wall Street-style day trading. These speculators aim to buy when prices are low and sell when they go up to make a quick profit (the "fast nickel"). Often the gains are smaller using this approach, but enough successful trades can add up quickly.

While trading between fiat and Bitcoin is one-way people can make (or lose) money, trades in the cryptocurrency space often involve exchanging one cryptocurrency for another rather than trading with fiat. Bitcoin is, in this context, sort of like the "gateway" cryptocurrency.

Trading Between Cryptocurrencies

There are hundreds of cryptocurrencies besides Bitcoin, with varying levels of value, volume, and potential. An active trading culture exists surrounding a number of these alternative currencies (often called "altcoins"). Some examples of popular altcoins include Ethereum, Litecoin, and Dogecoin. To buy into most altcoins, one usually needs to have Bitcoin, to begin with. Most altcoins cannot be purchased directly with fiat but rather with Bitcoin, although some exceptions exist.

The altcoin space is a bit of a "wild west," where high risks can lead to high rewards or big losses. Remember the early Bitcoin adopter who bought 2 pizzas? For many, the appeal of investing in altcoins is that they have the potential to increase dramatically in value as Bitcoin did. If an altcoin is backed by a promising application and strong development team, speculators may invest if they see the growth potential. Hedge funds have even begun to emerge, dealing exclusively in cryptocurrencies and blockchain technology.

The emerging paradigm of blockchain-based currencies and applications has led to a huge surge of speculative investment in this space, which in turn has led to an abundance of new "altcoins" competing to lead the way in different specialized use cases. Ethereum, for example, is widely seen as second to Bitcoin as the most popular cryptocurrency. Some believe that Ethereum will surpass Bitcoin in value and popularity and have hedged their "slow dime" bets by investing in Ethereum. Likewise, many have invested in other promising newcomers to the space and are willing to wait five years or more for the value to increase.

For serious investors interested in emerging technologies, the cryptocurrency and blockchain space beyond Bitcoin is extremely promising. Like many up-and-coming tech spaces, there is also a lot of noise to sift through. Everybody has an opinion on the future of blockchain technology, and obviously, they can't all be correct. Listening to others is a great way to learn, but it is up to you to form your own opinions and decide what's in your best interest.

Getting Paid in Bitcoin

Bitcoin's value and long-term viability largely depend on how many people are willing to accept it as a form of payment. With the recent rise in mainstream recognition, more and more vendors are offering to pay for goods and services with Bitcoin.

Historically, the volatility of Bitcoin has made many businesses reluctant to adopt it as a payment option. Today, however, more and more companies are integrating options for Bitcoin payment into their business model. You can now pay for things like plane tickets, online classes, cheeseburgers, and much more with a Bitcoin transaction.

For freelancers, small businesses, and entrepreneurs, getting paid in Bitcoin is one way to invest in the currency. If you get paid in Bitcoin for a service and the value of Bitcoin goes up more than the value of whatever fiat currency you would have otherwise been paid in, you can continue to earn even after the job is over. Of course, it bears repeating that the opposite could happen, as well. Many people set up wallets to accept tips in Bitcoin, which can be a fun way to get your feet wet without staking too much.

Bitcoin Faucets

If you spend some time online searching Bitcoin topics, you will likely come across a mention of Bitcoin "faucets." These are websites that you can visit to receive very small amounts of Bitcoin for free every so often. Most faucets operate by giving away a "trickle" of free Bitcoin while making money by showing ads on the webpage. Some faucets feature games, such as digital dice, which yield higher or lower rewards from the faucet. Generally speaking, you will not make very much money from faucets, although it can add up if you make a point of visiting every day over a long time.

5

STORY OF DOGECOIN AND SHIBA INU

"The market is a device for transferring money from the impatient to the patient." - Warren Buffet

Dogecoin is a cryptocurrency that was created as a joke in 2013. It was based on a Shiba Inu dog who talks in broken English, a common meme character.

In late 2013, software engineers Jackson Palmer and Billy Marcus founded Dogecoin. Palmer created the cryptocurrency's logo by misspelling "doge" to describe a Shiba Innu puppy, a common meme. "Doge began to make fun of Bitcoin," Pat White, CEO of Bitwave, said. In the beginning, a group of Dogecoin supporters organized promotional stunts to increase the currency's profile, such as raising funds to take the Jamaican Bobsleigh team to the 2014 Olympics or funding a NASCAR racer.

Jackson Palmer, an Adobe project manager, created a coin and website based on the meme dog. According to him, Billy Markus, a software designer, then programmed the digital currency, which took him about three hours. The aim was to make fun of the currency boom and people's willingness to spend on something they did not understand. Regrettably, this is precisely what occurred.

Dogecoin acquired cult status in early 2021 on Reddit's WallStreetBets message board—the primary catalyst for the GameStop incident in January—where supporters vowed to push its value "to the stars" (that was before all discussion of crypto was banned on the subreddit). Dogecoin is no longer a joke, with its value skyrocketing by more than 5,000 per cent in 2021. Tesla CEO Elon Musk is a supporter, calling Dogecoin his favourite cryptocurrency. Musk has dubbed Dogecoin the "people's crypto" and claimed that a physical Dogecoin token would be planted on the moon.

Dogecoin now has a market capitalization of $7 billion, comparable to several large-scale multinational companies. Dogecoin's value has risen by 2,400 per cent in the last year. Sceptics see this as proof that Dogecoin's worth can be exploited so quickly. Markus and Palmer also dropped Dogecoin in 2015, citing dubious traders and a hostile atmosphere as reasons.

Why is Everybody Talking About It?

Dogecoin's appeal stems in part from its amusement value. It has a sizable fan base, several of which are first-time investors. It has a devoted Reddit audience and is the focus of several amusing memes. Beginner investors are less intimidated and glad to be a club member because it does not take itself seriously. Mark Cuban, a billionaire capitalist, compares it to purchasing a lottery ticket with a low entry barrier. That is a good analogy.

He also informed Forbes that he purchased Dogecoin for his son to educate him about investing. "Dogecoin is less than a dime; you can buy $1 or $10 worth and have a good time watching it all day," he said. "I purchased a couple dollars' worth for my boy, and we watch it and talk about all of the price changes and why they happen; it is interesting, entertaining, and insightful for him."

Another factor people are curious about Dogecoin is Cuban's words: celebrity support. Elon Musk, the CEO of SpaceX and Tesla, is the most well-known supporter. Others also joined the Doge bandwagon, including Snoop Dogg, Mia Khalifa, and Gene Simmons. From "Who let the Doge out" to a spoof Vogue-Dogue magazine cover, the coin has a lighthearted tone that has contributed to its popularity.

What Is Dogecoin's Long-Term Future?

A lot of press speculation is also driving Dogecoin's price up. Elon Musk has joined in the fun. He began tweeting about it at the end of last year and has not yet stopped. The price of Dogecoin has been steadily that. However, with the coin's lack of utility, it is not easy to see it having a long-term future. There is no limit on Dogecoin, unlike certain other currencies. Dogecoins have a current supply of 128 billion.

Musk has tweeted several times about his enthusiasm for the coin. People will continue to purchase it as long as he continues to do so. Although joining the buzz on social media may be a good short-term trading tactic, it does not guarantee that DOGE would be a long-term hit.

Is it a Good Time to Invest in Dogecoin?

There is also little reason to keep Dogecoin for the long term since there is no lifetime cap on the amount of Dogecoins that will live, and millions of new Dogecoins are launched into the exchanges every day. Because of the system's lifetime limit on the number of coins that can be made, Bitcoin's value continues to grow. Doge is more like DASH or Bitcoin Cash than Bitcoin, where the express target is a spending currency.

Dogecoin's per-coin worth has historically been quite poor, hovering about $0.003 for much of 2020, meaning people were more inclined to give them away. Users on social media sites such as Twitter, Reddit, Facebook, and others will use Dogecoin to praise or "tip" each other for sharing content. The gains in Dogecoin that occurred in 2021 could not be sustainable in the long run. It remains to be seen if the cryptocurrency tipping and donation community can survive.

Shiba Inu Coin

Shiba Inu Coin has proved to be an excellent investment opportunity in the year 2020-2021. But how did this coin come into the picture?

In August 2020, an anonymous Indian by the name of Ryoshi created the Shiba Inu Coin. It is an altcoin of Dogecoin named after the Japanese dog breed, Shiba Inu. Like many other coins, the Shiba Inu coin was built on top of the Ethereum blockchain network. The coin is rising in popularity among investors and has already taken over some Dogecoin markets.

Shiba Inu is built on the ethereum network, while Dogecoin was developed using Bitcoin technology.

Shiba Inu has been popular for two primary reasons;

Elon Musk, Tesla founder, led to the increase of the Shiba Coin by 300%. This was through his expression of interest in owning up a Shiba Pup on Twitter.

Ethereum blockchain network founder, Vitalik Buterin, donated 50 trillion Shiba Coins to India. This was the covid relief fund of Sandeep Naiwal, an Indian crypto entrepreneur. The price of Shiba drastically fell up to 40% after this donation.

WHERE TO BUY Shiba Inu coins

Binance, crypto.com, Atomic wallet, KuCoin are some of the Crypto exchange platfowms where you can buy Shiba

Inu coins. You can also purchase Shib Coin on Uniswap Via Trust Wallet to exchange Ethereum for Shiba Coins.

Shiba Inu Price Prediction 2021 to 2022

Towards the end of August, the coin may had towards the previous highs of $0.0000090.

Expect the price to push towards the $0.00001 region in the next three months, representing a 30% increase from the current Shiba Inu price.

At the beginning of 2022, we predict the coin to be worth $0.000015. If this happens, it, therefore, means 91% returns if you invest today.

Where to invest Shiba Inu

The best crypto exchange for investing in Shiba Inu is eToro. e Toro is not technically an exchange but offers a cost-effective and easy way of investing in Shiba Inu. To ensure all platform traders are protected, e Toro is regulated by reputable organizations such as FCA, ASIC, and CySEC.

6

MEME COINS

"I have no special talent. I am only passionately curious." - Albert Einstein

Now it's time to discuss the crypto-craziness that is now taking place. Assume you were approached by someone who offered you the opportunity to risk any amount of money. You have a 50% risk of losing more than half of it, but a 50% chance of multiplying it by more than 100. This is the situation in which Meme coins are currently operating in the cryptocurrency market. As a result of DOGE's popularity, meme coins have emerged. Some have gained significant traction.

So What Is A Meme Coin?

A meme coin is a coin or a token that has no inherent value. In other words, there is no utility with meme coins. They are typically themed around a meme on the internet, but not limited to memes for example, dogecoin, the original meme coin that branded off the doge meme. Back then, creating a cryptocurrency was not so easy. You had to be a developer. You need to have a set of skills to create your cryptocurrency. Nowadays, what you need to do is pay the fee and sign up. And boom, you have your cryptocurrency. That is how meme coins are popping up every single day. All they do is pick a name, pay the fees, and provide liquidity.

The most difficult aspect of a meme coin, realistically, is persuading enough people that your coin is the next dogecoin. Because everyone knows that if you bought dogecoin when it was first released, you'd be laughing with the billionaires right now. As we previously mentioned, a cryptocurrency can be used for a variety of purposes. Meme coins, on the other hand, are mostly purchased for the sake of the meme. Utility isn't required for meme coins. When people buy the coin out of the liquidity pool, it gains value.

These meme coins often have an extremely large circulating quantity, ranging from one quadrillion to one hundred quadrillion. When you buy meme coins from the liquidity pool, the value rises since the supply in the liquidity pool decreases. This is a computerized version of a traditional exchange with a buyer and a seller. The advantages of a liquidity pool are that it makes it very easy for users to make trades even if the market size is small and the volume is low.

The concern is that it almost offers anyone the flexibility to simply toss their coin into the pool, causing the value to collapse. However, there are a few things to keep an eye out for.

What Has Happened Recently About Meme Coin?

The cryptocurrency market had a spectacular year in 2020-2021. There has been a huge growth in low market cap deflationary coins, especially in the last few months. A low market cap indicates that it is extremely undervalued and is often only beginning to deflate. The circulating supply will theoretically continue to decrease, enhancing the value each coin.

For example, in early March 2021, a token named Hoge Finance was gaining traction as the next dogecoin. They devised a brilliant strategy for accomplishing their goal.

They built this token with a liquidity pool, which means that every time you buy a coin, the circulating quantity decreases, and the value rises as long as there is a steady flow of buyers into the pool. Their token, on the other hand, had only one major flaw. They built it on the Ethereum network, which has extremely high gas fees, thus every time you transfer this Hoge token, you will pay a large gas fee. That was no pleasure for anyone, and it quickly lost steam and faded out. But, not long after, another coin appeared, addressing the fundamental issue by utilizing a different network with extremely cheap gas fees: $ 0.15 per transaction. Safemoon is the name of the token, which was developed on the Binance smart chain network. Many people considered Safemoon to be the next Hoge at this stage. This time, however, there is a lot more possibility for longevity

After people saw the early success of Safemoon, there were probably a hundred more copycats. It becomes a competition to see who can come up with the best branding and come up with some utility for your meme coin. Speaking of branding and utility, one of the more clever ones is this one called Elongate. Elon Musk, the CEO of Tesla, made a tweet saying, "if there is ever a scandal about me, please call it elongate." Within an hour, a new token called Elongate was entirely made for the meme hoping that Elon Musk might tweet about it one day.

The unique about them is that they put half into a donating wallet where they use that money for different charities. As of now, they have raised over 1 million dollars for charity just in April alone. There's been a couple of other charity tokens that have popped up, while Elongate seems to be the biggest and most successful one so far.

Now you may wonder: **Is It A Good Idea To Buy Meme Coins Now?**

There's no right answer. There's a lot of coins that could follow in the footsteps of Safemoon and Elongate, as well as many others that have been very successful. The biggest places to find them are TikTok and Reddit. You can also find them on Twitter. Since there's just a lot of momentum happening right now, and we are still at its early stage, you could easily double your money.

However, before you go ahead and buy a meme token, you need to know some risks.

The biggest risk is that there will be many scams because it is so easy to create your own meme token. The scam is what is called a rug pull. This is where the developers hold a bunch of coins and get people to buy-in, and then dump their coins back into the market, causing the value to plummet. They take their money and run. The best way to avoid this problem is to research and find validated, audited coins with a third-party safety check. If the developer is very public with who they are, they show their face or voice, and there's a good chance that the developer is not planning on scamming people because they essentially just doxed themselves. For example, there is a coin called 100x-Coin. The developer does daily live streams. He's very public with who he is and his intentions. It's unlikely that this is a rug pull. If a coin already has a lot of holders. For instance, if a meme coin has more than 100,000, or even into half a million holders, chances are it'd be challenging to pull the rug. So, try and do your best to figure out if this person is just shilling their coin or genuinely believe that their coin is the next dogecoin.

With that being said maybe, you're interested in and want to buy your meme coins; the next question is:

How to Buy Meme Coins?

First, you need a wallet, like the MetaMask wallet. Think of this as a physical wallet that when you go from website to website, you can take money from your wallet and use it on the website. By default, the MetaMask wallet is designed for Ethereum smart chain network or smart contract. But as mentioned earlier, we're not using the Ethereum network. We are using the Binance smart contract network, so we have to get the network information and configure it ourselves. It's not complicated. If you search on google "binance smart contract network MetaMask," navigate to this site, they make it pretty clear how to set up your Meta-Mask. Get your wallet set up with the Binance network.

Next, you need some BNB that is the coin we will be using to add to the liquidity pool to receive our meme tokens. Now the best way to get BNB coin is from Binance themselves.

Once you have acquired your BNB, you then want to send it to your MetaMask wallet. Now when doing this, we need to make sure that we are withdrawing on the BSc network. On Binance, hit withdraw, put in your address, and make sure it's sending on the BSc network, and that will transfer over to your wallet. Sometimes the transfer can be quick, but sometimes it can take up to an hour.

So, once you've got your BNB in your MetaMask wallet, go to Pancakeswap and look for the meme coins that are 99 percent available. Pancakeswap is a website that allows you to connect your MetaMask wallet and swap tokens for others. It also happens to be the most popular location for all meme coins. You probably won't be able to find the token you're looking for on the internet because it's not publicly available. All of these coins have a relatively little market capitalization. Almost none of them are listed in the public domain. You'll want to go to the coin's official website, where you'll most likely see a buy button. That buy button will most likely take you back to Pancakeswap with a URL that already contains the token address.

You should see a pop-up with a disclaimer letting you know that tokens can have the same name as others. So be careful, be sure that you are not being tricked, and buy the token you intend to purchase. Then, enter the amount of BNB you would like to swap, and you will receive your first meme token.

Now there is one more step you get to do, and you can either do this after or before you buy your token. You just want to add that token to your wallet. Don't worry. You won't see the coin you purchased yet if you bought the token and haven't added it to your wallet. But it is there on the blockchain and associated with your wallet address. You just have to add it to the display. So the best way to do this is to go up to the URL, copy the token address, open up your MetaMask wallet, add your token, hit the custom button, and paste in your address. You then should see your meme token in your wallet. Just a heads up, this can be pretty quick, but sometimes it can take a bit to appear. Also, you can always verify your token on BscScan, where you can find all the information that is going on with the BSc blockchain.

How To ACTUALLY Make Money from Meme Coins

Meme coins are where you can 10x your value or lose all your money in a day. You will likely lose all that money shortly after if you're greedy. That's why you should know what you're looking for. So here are some tips on making money with meme coins.

I. **Follow the hype but do not fall for the hype.**

A lot of these coins are pretty baseless. They don't have much of a model. There's no business plan, literally no utility. The value only comes when people buy and hope for the value to go up. So that being said, all these coins only run off hype if people are talking about it to cause their value to go up. For example, the Elongate, as we mentioned above. It became a cryptocurrency token within minutes of Elon Musk's tweet. So if you can manage to jump on those coins early, that can be a pretty good gamble but a terrible investment.

Another way coins build a lot of hype is when they say they're going to get listed on an exchange. Typically, when the coin gets listed on an exchange, it will get a big wave of new buyers, causing the price to go up, which is very much true. When the coin does get listed, that does happen, but typically, the price will also crash right after. Because there was all this hype, everybody was waiting for that one moment for the coin to get listed, the price goes up, and then suddenly everybody starts selling to take their profits. So be prepared if your coin starts to go up, and it's probably going to fall right after.

I. Don't get greedy. Take profit and play it safe.

It's okay if you don't sell your coin at the very top of the peak. Selling off a portion of your coins is a brilliant thing to do. For example, let's say you were at a peak, and you sold half your coins. Now one of two things is probably going to happen: it's either going to crash, or it's going to continue to run. If you sold half your coins, you would get the best of both worlds. If it falls, at least you sold half your coins; if it rises, you still got your half in there. It's smart to take profits.

That being said, don't put your faith in any particular coin. Sometimes, keep holding can also be a great strategy.

But odds are a lot of these tokens are probably going to die off. You're probably better off finding those coins with a lot of momentum and doing your best to jump in and jump out at the right times.

Another thing I would recommend is avoiding those big Telegram groups or Discord groups with like 50,000 or more than 100,000 people. More times than not, those groups are probably just "pump and dump" scams. You won't want to get caught in a pump and dump. A "pump and dump" is it's when you get a bunch of people or a bunch of money, and you pump it into a coin, the value goes flying, and then you sell all your coins. Meme coins are extra dangerous liquidity pools. Because it doesn't even require a buyer, you can just dump your money into the pool. So watch out for those types of groups. Similar "pump and dump" groups exist in Reddit too.

1. "Whale" watching.

A whale is somebody who has a lot of money that they're putting into crypto. Because crypto is all available information, you can just follow and see what they buy. For example, when Elon Musk tweeted Dogefather, a whale purchased a whole bunch of this coin, and if you followed and bought it. There's a high chance that you will make money from it.

But at the same time, you might find a whale that doesn't know what they're doing, and they just have a lot of money. So there's a risk of this strategy. So don't go buying that coin right away after you watch that whale buy. Maybe wait until at least there's a website or a Twitter page for that meme coin, then decide if it's a good idea to buy it. The last thing you will want is to panic buy and then get the rug pulled.

I. **Holding.**

If you get in at the right point, this strategy can be the most effective. For example, if you got in very early on Safemoon, you probably have made a lot of money just by holding it. The only issue is that you need to know when to stop holding. Most of the time, it can be even better if you sold and found other coins that had more potential and less risk of falling. We will talk more about when to exit your position in the later chapters. Here is a quick way to check the risk of rewarding ratio if you keep holding that coin. Let's say, if your coin had a big run already, and you see that its highest price is about five times compared to its current price, and its' lowest price is 50% of its current price. This is mean the potential profit could be five times, but you can also lose 50%. It could be a good idea to hold it a little bit longer in this case.

The bottom line is that it needs your research, and it can take a lot of time to find a profitable meme coin. Always remember to manage your risk.

WHAT ARE ALTCOINS?

An Altcoin is simply any cryptocurrency besides bitcoin. Bitcoin launched in 2009, very soon after developers started trying to improve upon bitcoin and create entirely new currencies with new use cases. That's how we got all the cryptocurrencies we have today. Some of you may have heard of Litecoin, Ethereum, Bitcoin Cash, or other popular altcoins.

The world of altcoins is truly amazing... and it's all due to the creation of blockchain technology and the grandfather of crypto currency... BITCOIN.

The first altcoins to come onto the scene in the early

days of bitcoin are Etherium and Litecoin. Etherium is multi-faceted and used to create "smart contracts" with hundreds if not thousands of applications.

It also serves as a type of "fuel" for doing crytpo transactions.

Litecoin is a fork of the original bitcoin blockchain and was created to be used as an everyday spending type of currency instead of bitcoin, which many use to store larger amounts of bitcoin in a hard wallet or exchange. If you think of your Bitcoin wallet as a bank, then Litecoin would be the pocket money you carry around.

There are hundreds and even thousands of different altcoins now... each with its intended purpose. Z-cash provides greater security, XYO promises to be the world's first competition for GPS, yet others deal in shopping, transferring assets globally with lightening speed and inexpensively, and creating more efficient communication, safety, and accountability for crypto currency transactions.

If you are interested in learning about individual altcoins, check out www.coinmarketcap.com as a resource to search for and research various coins in depth. How, where, who, and why can all be answered quickly and easily using the website.

What Are the Best Altcoins to Own?

These are altcoins that I hold and continue to watch and trade. There are many choices available and everyone should do their research to learn about and get behind the technology and application of the coin or token that resonates and makes sense to them.

Bitcoin

This is the first cryptocurrency ever to be created and is still the most popular today. Bitcoin was launched in 2009 by an individual or group of individuals who go by the name

Satoshi Nakamoto (the true identity of this person remains unknown).

The network requires users to use a blockchain to make transactions, and new bitcoins are created through mining. These bitcoins can then be sold for cash or used to make purchases on an ever-growing number of online stores that now accept bitcoin as payment.

Ethereum

This is a new type of cryptocurrency introduced in 2015 and has rapidly grown in popularity due to its ease of use and large active user base. The network is built on the blockchain and uses ether – a cryptocurrency token –to make transactions.

This type of cryptocurrency can be used to build decentralized applications and is popular among developers because of the ease with which this can be done. In addition to this, the network has smart contracts built in, allowing you to create your own rules for transactions and automate making them.

Monero

Monero was created as a more secure alternative to bitcoin, with the main difference being that transactions are completely anonymous and cannot be traced. The network uses a special kind of cryptography called CryptoNote to achieve this and is also completely decentralised.

Dash

This network is very similar to bitcoin, but it has been designed specifically for point-of-sale purchases. The cryptocurrency was launched in 2014 by Evan Duffield after he noticed that bitcoin had some serious limitations when it came to being used as an actual currency. Dash is very popular among merchants because of its speed and efficiency when making point-of-sale purchases.

IOTA

This network was created in 2015 and is designed specifically for the Internet of Things ("IoT," which refers to the growing number of internet-enabled devices that we use today). IOTA uses a unique technology called Tangle to make transactions – this is quite different from blockchain technology that most other cryptocurrencies use. This network has been specifically designed for the IoT, which means that it can be used to securely and quickly make point-of-sale purchases.

Litecoin

This network was created by Charlie Lee in 2011 and is very similar to bitcoin. The main difference between the two coins is that litecoin has more coins available (84 million versus bitcoin 21 million) and faster block generation times (2.5 minutes versus 10 minutes). Despite these similarities, litecoin also has some key features that differentiate it from bitcoin. For example, litecoin uses a different proof of work algorithm called Scrypt, has a four-times larger block size, and offers quicker transaction confirmation times.

Ripple

This is a relatively new network that was created in 2012 by Chris Larsen and Jed McCaleb. The network is designed to transfer any currency (not just cryptocurrencies) and uses a unique technology called the Ripple Protocol consensus algorithm to achieve this. The platform has attracted a lot of attention because it also features fast transaction speeds and can transfer any currency – including pounds, euros, yen, or even US dollars. It can also be used to transfer any of the hundred-plus currencies that are available on the network. This makes it very easy for banks and other financial institutions to use Ripple to alternative traditional payment methods like SWIFT.

7

ICOS AND SCAMS

"We simply attempt to be fearful when others are greedy and to be greedy only when others are fearful." - Warren Buffet

An Initial Coin Offering (ICO) is a method for fundraising that trades future crypto coins for liquid cryptocurrencies. It is, however, a very risky way to raise funds. It is not advisable to invest in anything that you cannot afford to lose. Remember that you can have a hard time getting back the money you have lost if you fail.

Anyway, an ICO is a crowd sale, which is a cryptocurrency for crowdfunding. It is similar to the Initial Public Offering (IPO), except it sells tokens on the blockchain instead of selling shares. It occurs before the launch of this blockchain. It also involves a crowd sale or public sale of a coin's initial supply.

An Initial Coin Offering is sometimes called an Initial Public Coin Offering (ICPO) or Initial Token Offering (ITO). Other people even call it a Crypto Crowdsale. As for the startups, they are referred to as Blockchain Startups.

Most companies that perform ICOs offer tokens instead of coins. You should know the difference between these two. Coins are used to transfer monetary value, while tokens are used to store multifaceted and complex data streams.

Likewise, most companies that hold ICOs are built on a blockchain. Hence, they cannot be simply judged based on their monetary value. They have to be assessed according to their solution and business model.

How about the ICO 'white paper'? All ICO's need to have a manifesto or a white paper. It should explain in detail how the technology functions as well as how tokens are designed. It should also explain how users can obtain and use such tokens.

If you want to find out more about certain founders and their work, you can use white paper. It will tell you whether these founders have thought through their project or not. It will also tell you about the problems it can solve and how they can be solved.

How ICO's Work

In essence, an ICO works according to the following:

1. The startup releases an advertisement regarding the selling of its new cryptocurrency's initial coin supply.
2. The investors read the startup's white paper, who eventually exchange Ether or Bitcoin for new coins.
3. The startup can exchange your Ether or Bitcoin into regular fiat currency to pay for the costs of building out the technology.
4. If the project launches successfully, the new currency's value goes up and the investors profit.

Companies use ICO because it gives them a faster and

easier way to fundraising for a new blockchain project. Also, it is border-free. So, it can connect to all the possible investors worldwide. More often than not, some of the tokens are sold to the participants of ICO while the others are kept for the company's needs.

What are examples of companies that used ICO for project fundraising? Well, there's Bancor, which raised $150 million in less than three hours. There's also BAT, which raised $34 million in less than one minute. Then, there's Tezos. It raised $232 million in just one month.

ICO truly sounds fascinating. How do investors make money from it? A lot of investors believe that the startup would be successful in launching on an exchange. They anticipate such success to sell coins or tokens as soon as possible to earn a profit. Most of the time, they do not believe in the company. They may believe in its idea, but not enough to risk going in for the long haul if earning big is not feasible in the short term.

ICO-Issued Coins and Tokens

Coins and tokens that have been issued in an ICO have three main roles:

1. They represent the product of the company. They can be used as an exchange medium for a specific amount of services or products. They can also be used for project trading.
2. They represent the right to share profits. Just like regular shares, coins can be shared by the company.
3. They represent the product of the company. Coins may be used as a means of exchange for a specific amount of services or products. They can also be used as a means to trade in a project.
4. They represent profit-sharing rights. Just like

regular shares, coins can be shared at a certain percentage.

5. They represent corporate bonds. Coins can function just like loans. The owner can acquire interest depending on the pre-set rate.

The Disadvantages of ICO Investments

ICO's seem great, but just like everything else, they also have disadvantages. For starters, the concept of the startup is on "white paper." There isn't any evidence of work. Investors mainly rely on this white paper for information. Thus, they become susceptible to fraud.

These fraudsters make people believe that they can become rich if they invest in ICO's. However, they do not follow through with their promises. Once they get the money, they go on their way. They do not produce any product.

For example, Mycelium ICO was a huge failure for investors. After acquiring funding, the members of the team just disappeared. It was later discovered that they used the money to have a vacation.

Another disadvantage of ICO's is that some legitimate companies do not have the right technical support and knowledge. They may intend to produce products, but they lack the necessary knowledge and experience to build a blockchain business.

For example, CoinDash was a disaster for its investors. Millions of dollars were lost when hackers were able to make their way through the company's website. The hackers replaced the ICO wallet address with their own.

How to Invest In ICO

If, after learning about the disadvantages of investing in

ICO, you still want to go into this venture, here are the things that you have to keep in mind:

Always do your research.

Staying up to date with the latest trends and news is vital for any business. However, this is especially important for ICO investments. As you know, ICO's are startups that need funding to grow. Without investors, their theories cannot be put into practice. Hence, you should do your research meticulously. Use the Internet to your advantage and learn everything you can about cryptocurrencies and ICO's.

Find out if the team is able to deliver. Read the white paper thoroughly before going to the team members and the founders. Use the Internet to obtain more information. For instance, you can use LinkedIn to learn more about them. Check out what is written on their profiles to know more about their credibility.

Do your research about the team and find out if the members have any experience on cryptocurrency, projects, and ICO's. Learn as much as you can, specifically on their involvement. If you think that they can deliver the results you want, you can do more research.

Be meticulous about your research. Make sure that you find out if they are merely scammers or fraudsters. You can join groups or forums for like-minded individuals. You can read their posts or send them questions.

Consider the thoughts of experienced investors.

Ask yourself if their thoughts do solve problems or if there is any validity in their ideas. Consider if their ideas target a potential market and can lead to success. Ask yourself what values their projects can bring to society. Are these people offering new concepts, or are they merely offering something that has already been developed? Ponder the answers. Do not invest unless you fully believe that the team can do things better.

Find out what the tokens are for.

With ICO's, new tokens are created for a project. Every project should state what the tokens are for. For example, ask why Ethereum or Bitcoin are not enough to function as tokens for the project.

Find out how much money is being obtained.

In the past, some ICO's were able to collect an unlimited sum of money. The investors were given open caps that allowed them to send unlimited funding to projects. In general, the more coins circulate, the less unique the tokens become for trading.

In addition, you have to find out what the team uses the money for and how much they allot for development and marketing budgets. Do not forget to find out how much they allot for essential allocations. Remember that a good ICO is transparent and lets investors know where their money goes.

Know the token value.

How much are the tokens currently worth? As an investor, you want to know if your tokens would grow in value over the next few years. You also want to know if there is a chance for the market to be saturated by such tokens. Moreover, you want to know about the incentives involved in these tokens. After all, you can only earn a profit if your tokens grow in value.

Learn how and when tokens are distributed.

If the team members are greedy, more than half of the tokens would be suspiciously distributed. This is why you have to know how and when the tokens would be distributed. Good projects link their token distributions to roadmaps because every milestone requires a specific amount of funding.

See to it that you also monitor the stage when tokens are distributed. Certain projects only release tokens when the

ICO has ended. Conversely, certain projects have to have beta versions before sending out tokens. Then again, even though learning about these things is helpful, they should still not affect your decision to invest.

Exchange Fiat Currency for Cryptocurrency

For you to be able to take part in ICO's, you need cryptocurrencies. The most popular ones are Ethereum and Bitcoin. Take note that the startup exchanges investment money for fiat currency to pay for costs and developments, among others.

ICO Investment

When the startup asks you to send cryptocurrencies to a specific address, consider that many startups do not accept Ether and Bitcoin. Some exchanges do not send these cryptocurrencies to ICO startups. Usually, they are sent from online wallets.

Follow the Startup Development

Lots of individuals simply leave their money in startups and hope for the best. While there is nothing wrong with doing this, you may want to exert more effort to get the best results. After all, cryptocurrency investments are a huge deal. Unless you want to lose your hard-earned money, you should not take things lightly.

Cryptocurrency trading is very risky and speculative. So, it is wise to spread out your risks. This way, you can minimize your odds of losing. Moreover, it would help if you exerted more effort in knowing more about the startups that you follow. Read the news. Browse the Internet. Communicate with like-minded individuals who may be of help.

You can also go to conferences and meet the team. Talk to them. Send them emails. Find out their reactions. Get acquainted with these people because they may be able to help you out.

8

PROTECT YOUR CRYPTO INVESTMENT AGAINST THEFT AND HACK

"Once we accept our limits, we go beyond them." - Albert Einstein

I n the world of the web in general and particularly that of cryptocurrencies, it is very important to protect yourself and raise your security levels because scams are prevalent. It would help if you always secured yourself and your investments. The Main Scams Related to Cryptocurrencies include:

Automated Trading Systems

Let us start with the most notorious Cryptocurrency scam, which is related to Automated Trading Systems.

Such scam traders have the sole interest in getting you to pour your capital into the coffers of an unregulated broker, usually on offshore territories, where your money becomes unrecoverable. Their only goal is to take a percentage of your deposited capital.

Phishing scams

Phishing is the illegal act of obtaining sensitive, confidential details such as usernames or passwords through camouflaging websites, etc. Users are fooled into thinking they are entering the information on a trusted website or a link that has been shared with them through emails or Google ads. What happens is that users are sent an email giving them the false idea that something has happened to their account or wallet and that they need to make it right by following a link. The link directs to a fake website, mostly resembling the original website with the same design, color schemes, and font style, forcing visitors to think they are right.

Once the user enters the information, it is passed onto the scammers, who then use it the way they want to. Depending upon the upside potential, they can use the information straight away or store it for later use.

Myetherwallet is a prime example of this style of scam. A fake website was designed with the same design and looked like the official website, making the users provide the information they would on the original platform. This resulted in considerable losses to the users.

To think that the fake Myetherwallet app became one of the top 3 apps on the app store. How easily it spread and affected so many users shows how vulnerable this industry can be and how vulnerable and prone to attacks users can be.

Another method is the use of airdrops. It's when fake companies pretend to be legitimate ones that offer free tokens to many people. Along them comes the need to download some app or a portal created by the same individuals looking to make easy money at your expense. They must enter the password and the usernames, exposing the private and the public keys, which enables the draining of the accounts.

DAO theft.

On the net, some DAO (decentralized autonomous organizations) have successfully issued their own crypto currencies. These systems can be an excellent earning system, especially if at the beginning we have little money to invest and can't afford a too famous virtual currency. Unfortunately, however, these systems are less secure. In 2016, for example, a DAO system was tampered with by a hacker who stole a third of the group's total coins on their account.

Abusive Cryptomining

In the world, one in five companies is affected by hacker attacks that exploit the computing power of unsuspecting users' personal computers to generate cryptocurrency, using other people's energy and facilities. To mine and earn cryptocurrency, it is necessary to use powerful computers in both core and graphics card structure, operating 24 hours a day, seven days a week. A side aspect of mining is that it consumes a lot of electricity (think of having many computers 365 days a year in perpetual operation).

Mining Scams

Mining scams are another exciting aspect of the scams. They use cloud mining. Now, not all cloud mining is illegitimate. Some use cloud mining for legitimate purposes. But like always, there are a few who have used cloud mining negatively and have carried out elaborate schemes to scam people.

Cloud mining is the process of mining bitcoins via a cloud. Here are companies that let people open an account with them, and in return, they let the users participate in the mining process. The process is conducted on a cloud, hence eliminating the cost of equipment maintenance and energy.

There are some out there offering completely legitimate operations, and people are being a part of it. But at the same time, there are companies out there that are totally on the wrong side of the law and ethical boundary. One way of looking at these operations and judging whether they will sting you or not. If the returns seem profitable, there is a chance it's totally fine, and there is nothing to worry about. But if there are no or very minimal returns, then that's a red flag. Steer clear of such setups. They aren't for you. Or anyone, for that matter.

Transparency is very important. Every user has the right to know everything about the company they are going to be involved with. There should be no question about it. Is the setup allowing free scrutiny of the way they work, what tools they utilize, and how they are planning to take the business forward, then you should be pretty sure that there is something that they do not want you or anyone outside of the inner circle to know.

Malware Scams

A malware portal is used to infect your pc, and it hits right where it needs to in your space. Malicious software is created. Now once the computer is infected, the virus takes over, and it can operate and take out the private information or data in a way it was designed to do.

There are numerous ways through which the job can be done.

An example is that that it can compromise your BTC wallet. When you attempt to send some coins to a friend in need, the original address may be replaced with a fake one that belongs to the scammer.

A type of malware scam that saw itself get noticed was called the Crypto Currency Clipboard Hijackers. They used the Windows clipboard as a weapon. Now some of these scammers used the windows clipboard to monitor a few thousand cryptocurrency addresses, but this one was pretty big. This one that was reported by some leading news portals used to monitor some 2.3 million addresses.

They use the copy-paste mechanism of the Windows systems. As the addresses are usually long and difficult to remember, when the users copy and paste the addresses, the scammers would replace the addresses with the forged ones. And the transactions would land in the wrong hands.

Here's how to spot such an activity

- Your pc slows signs of slowing down
- The pop ads, well, they pop up, but there are too many to the point they begin to annoy
- You also may notice some unusual activity that you weren't responsible for

Fake Wallets

Fake wallets are also a favorite of scammers. They create a fake wallet to trick people into revealing their passwords and keys. Bitcoin gold was new to the market, and users looking to stake a claim were led on a fake wallet that went by the name of "mybtgwallet.com." Thinking this was the real thing, users provided their information regarding their private keys. And were deprived of millions of dollars as a result.

This scam emptied pockets and cost the users a combined amount that nears $3.5 million

Keeping in mind the amount of fake Google ads and advertisements thrown at you every day, you have to be very careful when visiting a website. The ideal thing to keep the original website that you use bookmarked or type the address manually in your browser.

Here's how to spot such a scam

- The information about the model is not there
- There is no presence of it on big media outlets usually covering every aspect of this world
- The platform has been newly formed

- You don't see "Https." Instead, there's just "Http"(
  meaning the connection isn't secure)

ICO Scams

ICO is an Initial coin offering that the developers or the creators conduct to raise money for their company or the startup. Since the main reason to conduct ICOs is to raise money, the motive behind the money-raising activity is essential. It may differ sometimes. Some groups conduct ICOs, and they are serious about what they will do with the money.

Since the money is raised, and there is no regulatory body to check what they choose to do with the money, they are free to decide what happens and what doesn't. They can vanish onto thin air with the money, or they can go the other direction and work within the legal confines.

A study conducted by the Wall Street Journal states that 1 in 5 Initial Coin Offerings [ICO] shows hints of fraudulent activates. That's 18.6%. That's a big chunk of the total ICOs conducted, and it did impact the market. Somewhere, somehow people were attached and involved in any capacity with these ICOs conducted.

ICOs are carried out to bypass the arduous process of finding capital investment through banks or VC capitalism. There is a massive surge in the amounts being raised by ICOs in the year 2018. The first 5 months of the year 2018 doubled the total of last year's total.

This trend shows that the bigger this segment of the crypto currency world gets, the chances of it getting affected by scammers and fraudsters are likely to get higher.

A Prime example of an ICO scam is the Giza Scam. Almost $2 million were looted.

The project showed signs of warnings when the main supplier, which was supposed to develop their device, announced it had cut ties with Giza, citing alarming reasons for the audience. They alleged that the project seemed to be a scam. And they weren't in cooperation anymore.

The supplier company, The Third Pin, whose CEO Ivan Larionov, announced on a bit coin forum that his company has decided to cut ties with Giza. The explanation was as simple as that the Giza Honcho, known as Marco Fike, was unable to be clear throughout the negotiations, which was a major red flag. Referencing a particular point in time during the whole process, he specifically said that when inquired about when the device was supposed to roll out, Marco Fike failed to describe what he wanted to do and his plan. It indicated that the plan suggested publicly hadn't been worked out properly because the intention wasn't there at all. There was no seriousness and sincerity behind all the façade.

That's when the sole supplier decided to part ways with Giza. And this was the first blow in a series of many.

Soon after, the accounts began to dry up. Amounts had been transferred to other addresses.

Ponzi Schemes

These types of scams are exactly what the name suggests. We have all heard about how the Ponzi works. This classic scam technique is being used by traditional scammers who just can't get enough of their underhanded tactics. Very quickly, they invaded the cryptocurrency landscape and put the world on notice.

Ponzi schemes take money from you, promising to multiply it, which they do sometimes by asking you to refer colleagues and family. The second-tier influx brings about the capital to return the wealth of those who came first. However, the newer investors are rarely lucky when it comes to wealth being returned, multiplied because the scheme has been stopped on fraud and deceit. Did I mention that investment is made on a non-existent entity? Which means there wasn't any mechanism in the first place to multiply wealth other than grabbing money from the later investors who have been referred to them by YOU?

Sounds nice and warm!

These schemes run as long as the cat isn't out of the bag. The sooner the investors find out that they have been investing in a property or product that does not exist anywhere globally, the more likely they will demand a return. Which never goes smoothly? By now, it's already too late. Most of the money has been transported to foreign lands, laundered, or been used to fund any illegal activities, or it can be anywhere in the world. It doesn't matter where the money is or how it's been used; what matters is by then, people have been ripped off. The extent of the damage inflicted can be measured, but the effect it had cannot.

- How to Spot a Ponzi scam
- The revenue is exponentially high
- The success is dependent on referrals
- The business model feels incomplete
- Lack of transparency and lack of information of the company and the team behind it

These indicators are usually not very hard to find. If one may look with a keen eye and just a little bit of effort on your part, may expose a scheme before it's too late.

DeFi Rug Pulls

This is quite a new scamming strategy that has hit the cryptocurrency markets. This is when DeFi (decentralized finance) focuses on removing the gatekeepers of financial transactions. But this comes with it's own massive set of issues. Such bad actors have managed to get away with the funds of investors using these avenues. It is a practice that is normally called a 'rug pull.' Normally, what happens is a project is designed with the promise of great returns. The money is kept 'safe' in smart contracts. But programmers find ways to steal the fund after the contract expires or actually reaches the threshold limit, making use of the functions on the DeFi platform.

In December 2020, a group of developers stole almost $750,000 worth of Bitcoin and other cryptocurrencies. The project had promised to deposit their crypto in a locked smart contract, and the contract could only be executed after a very specific period of time. But the developers had developed and built in a back door and made away with the funds long before the smart contract had even expired.

How to avoid being scammed?

Now the question is what needs to be done to avoid such activities. The answer to that is to be informed. Keep yourself up to date. The more we know about what's happening around the world, the better.

- Subscribe to the news and read as much as possible. Keep yourself informed. Discuss with people who know about the subject and talk about it. It requires effort on your part. Be curious. Know more.
- Make sure the website address you are visiting in such a situation is what you always see. Usually, a few little differences are ignored or are hard to notice. But this is your hard-earned money we are talking about here. So you have to be careful every single time you are asked to enter your details. Double-check the address.

- It has to start with "https" and not just "http."
- Go with the gut feeling: If the website doesn't feel right, something looks off or feels different from routine. STOP! Do NOT proceed without verifying! Call a friend who knows a thing or two. Do something! Just don't go with the flow.
- Another very common tactic these fishy websites use is that use a sense of urgency. They give warnings. They use deadlines. They force the user to take action as quickly as possible with big, bold red titles with the text "HURRY" flashing like a traffic signal inciting panic and emergency in their minds. This forces the users to take quick action without reasoning, and 99 times out of 100, that is terrible.
- Always set a strong password.
- More importantly, REMEMBER that password. Commonly, people forget their passwords, and they cannot access their wallets.

EXAMPLES OF CRYPTO Scams And Hacks

News of security breaches at crypto exchanges can impact user confidence of the cryptocurrency market as a whole. The most famous hack occurred at the Mt Gox exchange in Japan in February 2014. This exchange alone was responsible for 70 percent of global Bitcoin transactions at the time. After suspending trading, the exchange became insolvent, having lost about 7000 Bitcoins in the hack attacks. This reality is a serious concern for any investor. Although it's currently a rare occurrence in 2021, it can immediately impact the value of many coins.

In 2016, Ethereum faced an existential crisis that would

determine how it would function in the future. A hack occurred on the Ethereum blockchain, targeting the decentralized autonomous organization (DAO), a fund built by Ethereum investors as a decentralized concept to invest in companies. The hacker, who remains unidentified, took off with $50 million worth of ether. This left Ethereum developers with two options: to continue accepting that the thief would now own a large percentage of ethers or create a hard fork that would disavow the hack, acting as if nothing happened. Ethereum developers ended up siding with the latter, moving the ether with the hard fork. Not everyone agreed with that solution, including Charles Hoskinson, one of Ethereum's cofounders. Those that remained on the original Ethereum blockchain, which concedes the hack, became Ethereum classic.

On the 10th of August 2021, a blockchain-based platform poly network was breached by hackers and stole $600 million in cryptocurrencies. This was allegedly one of the biggest ever hacks in crypto history.

9

NFTS

"The people who are crazy enough to think they can change the world are the ones who do." - Steve Jobs.

Crypto is all about decentralization. It is a type of technology that is slowly making its way into our daily lives. And what is decentralized technology? Well, the answer to that question can be quite complex. But we can take a look at it as something that has no central authority or governing body. In other words, it's a type of technology that is owned by the people and not a company or organization.

With this in mind, we can easily see how the concept of NFTs makes sense within the realm of crypto.

Let's take a look at the history of NFTs and how they came to be.

Where and when did NFTs first appear?

NFTs have become very popular in recent years, and they're going to be a big part of the future of crypto. But, where did they come from? Well, it all started with the idea that was thought up by a man named Nick Szabo.

Nick Szabo is an American computer scientist and cryptographer who has been credited with the creation of the first-ever smart contract. This contract was based on "The Fermi Paradox," which he designed back in 1995.

In this game, users would send a digital asset to another user without using any third-party services like banks or PayPal. To do this, you would need to send the digital asset to an anonymous public key address and then hope that it made its way to the intended recipient. If it didn't make its way there, then you would have lost your money forever unless someone else sent it to them for you.

The NFTs of Today

With this in mind, we can see how Nick Szabo came up with the idea for NFTs long before crypto was even around. Nowadays, many different types of NFTs being used in various industries and projects throughout the world. The biggest names in NFTs include CryptoKitties, Etheremon, and CryptoPunks.

These are just a few of the projects that have made their mark on the world of NFTs. There are many more out there that you can find on sites like Enjin. Enjin is a platform that is built specifically for creating and trading NFTs. It's like an online store where you can buy and sell various digital assets.

Now, it's important to note that these digital assets are not real-world items, they're based on blockchain technology and therefore cannot be touched or seen by the naked eye. However, some NFTs have physical representations as well, such as CryptoPunks or GigaPets from Rare Bits.

Etheremon is another popular NFT project that uses blockchain technology to create digital monsters based on the Ethereum blockchain. These monsters can be used in battle and are completely unique, so there is no way to get them again once they're sold or traded.

The popularity of NFTs is growing every day, and it seems like they're here to stay. Many companies are getting into the space by launching their own NFT projects. But, it's important to remember that these projects can be very confusing and risky for investors who don't understand how blockchain technology works.

CryptoKitties

CryptoKitties is a blockchain-based game that lets you buy, sell, and breed virtual cats. It was created by Axiom Zen, a Canadian company based in Vancouver. The game became popular with the release of CryptoKitties in November 2017.

CryptoKitties is a prime example of how NFTs can be used to create decentralized applications (DApps). It is one of the first games to use blockchain technology and is the best example of how it can create something enjoyable for the public.

The main goal of CryptoKitties is to breed rare cats that are valuable in the marketplace. You start out with two cats that you can then breed together and hope for rare offspring.

Many things make CryptoKitties a great game. The most important of these is the fact that it's fun to play. It's an inter-active game that lets you create new virtual cats with unique features and attributes. This makes it more than just a game. It is a tool for creative expression, as well as an investment opportunity.

If you're new to the crypto space, you may be wondering how exactly CryptoKitties work.

How Does CryptoKitties Work?

CryptoKitties works through the use of smart contracts on the Ethereum blockchain. This means that the Kitties are owned by their owners and not by anyone else. You can buy, sell, or breed your kitties on the marketplace, and no one can stop you from doing so. All transactions are recorded on the blockchain, and there is no central authority in charge of them.

In addition to this, each Kitty has its own set of unique characteristics or traits. These traits include color, pattern, eyes color, and coat pattern, which are randomly generated when a new Kitty is created on the blockchain platform. These traits can be passed down from parent to child during breeding sessions, resulting in new traits and combinations.

All of these traits and their values are recorded on the blockchain. This means that they cannot be tampered with or changed in any way. And because their owners own the kitties, no central authority can decide to take them away from you.

How Do You Buy CryptoKitties?

The first thing you need to do if you want to buy a CryptoKitty is to create an account on the platform. Once you've done this, you can then visit the marketplace and purchase a Kitty from one of the sellers there. You will then be given a private key that you can use to access your Kitty on the blockchain.

This private key is unique to your account and only works with your specific Kitty. So, if someone else has access to it, they won't be able to access your Kitty, even if they have an identical one of their own! This means that there is no way for anyone else but you to get hold of your Kitty without your permission.

How Much Are CryptoKitties Worth?

When CryptoKitties first launched, their price was relatively low compared to how much they are worth today. At first, they were only worth around $10 each, which made them accessible for just about anyone who wanted one! And with more and more people getting involved with CryptoKitties each day, their value has increased considerably.

Today, a single CryptoKitty can be worth anywhere between $100 and $20,000. And with more people becoming interested in them each day, their value will only increase in the future. So, if you're thinking about getting involved with CryptoKitties, now is the perfect time to do so!

Are CryptoKitties Legal?

Yes, it is completely legal to own a CryptoKitty, and they are completely legal on the blockchain platform that they run on. They have been deemed as an investment asset by the United States Securities and Exchange Commission (SEC) which means that you must be at least 18 years old to purchase one. This means that it is also illegal for anyone under 18 years old to buy a CryptoKitty! In addition to this, it is illegal for anyone who does not have access to their own private key (and the associated Kitty) to purchase one of these Kitties. So, if you're thinking about buying a Kitty for someone else as a gift, make sure that they are at least 18 years old before doing so!

Teens and Millennials successful stories

Randi Hipper, a 17-year-old senior at Xaverian High School in New York City, began producing her own digital artworks. She had heard about NFTs on Twitter and other social media channels.

She creates the concepts and collaborates with Ajay Toons, a teen lad from India known as, to sell the pieces on the NFT marketplace Atomic Hub. A nonfungible token, often known as an NFT, is a digital file formed using blockchain computer code. It's purchased with a cryptocurrency like Ether or Wax and exists as a one-of-a-kind file that can't be reproduced, usually merely to be admired digitally.

Beeple, a 40-year-old digital artist made news this spring when one of his paintings sold for sixty nine million dollars at Christie's. However, NFT platforms like Atomic Hub,

Nefty Blocks, and OpenSea are brimming with creators who are barely old enough to drive. They promote their art on social media rather than through high-end galleries or auction houses.

Nifty Gateway released a new product named Nifty Next Generation in June. It included pieces by jstngraphics, a 17-year-old from Washington state, and Solace, an 18-year-old from Soledad, California. Both youngsters created NFT art for less than a year and gained notoriety by selling their work on the internet auction site SuperRare. Both artists' paintings, which varied in price from roughly $1,000 to $7,250, were sold out.

Carlos Gomez, also known as Solace, began generating NFTs on a leased iPad. Solace and jstngraphics look like dinosaurs in comparison to Benyamin Ahmed, a 12-year-old boy from suburban London who produced an NFT collection last month. Weird Whales was a project that included 3,350 pixelated whales, each with their own set of characteristics, some of which were uncommon and hence more costly. Ahmed earned tens of thousands of dollars in bitcoin as a result of the collecting.

Such unlikely success tales have sparked the interest of enterprising young individuals to join the NFT craze. It's a fun after-school activity for some. Others see it as a stepping stone toward a full-time job as an artist or a crypto entrepreneur.

Magnus Aske, a 19-year-old student at Babson College in Wellesley, Massachusetts, contracted COVID-19 about the time of the Beeple auction last March. During his ten days in quarantine, he learned everything he could about NFTs and devised a plan to work with a foreign country's antiquities collection (his classmate had connections within the government).

Cubby, an online marketplace where college students

can sell their paintings, was founded by Josh Kim, a rising senior at Colby College. Kim plans to launch NFTs in the coming months, claiming that they will aid the site's goal of supporting young artists in "reaching financial success," or at the very least earning additional money while in school.

Making NFTs and other forms of digital art has become a modern take on grocery shopping or working at a fast-food restaurant for some teenagers. A 15-year-old in New York City produces custom artwork for Twitch users, a prominent gaming livestreaming network.

Victor Langlois, an 18-year-old transgender known as FEWOCiOUS, or Fewo to his admirers has done so well as an NFT artist. He does digital art that depicts his traumatic upbringing, gender identity struggles, and transition.

Last summer, Fewo began selling his work on Super-Rare, where he immediately established a following, as well as on Nifty Gateway. He soon got the attention of Noah Davis, a Christie's digital art specialist, who planned an auction of his work in June. Langlois shot to fame after a $2.16 million online auction with five pieces titled Hello, I'm Victor (FEWOCiOUS) and This Is My Life.

How to Create, Buy and Sell NFTs
How To Create NFT

I know you'll have questions about whether or not NFTs are worthwhile. Consider, for a moment, the world of traditional art. You see art galleries and people paying hundreds of thousands or millions of dollars for artwork, and then reality hits you. Under the right conditions, only a very few will make a living doing it. Even then, they must divide the benefits with other parties involved in the deal.

NFTs live in a special environment. You, the artist, have complete control over all of the strings that make up your work. NFT marketplaces are foreign marketplaces that display your work to the entire world. To sell your work, you don't need to go to a gallery or an agency. You are not forced to share a portion of your earnings with intermediaries.

NFT marketplaces, in reality, keep you updated on the selling of your artwork at all times. You can earn a reasonable commission from your artwork's NFT once it is traded.

You may also prove the validity of your work at any time and that there is only one true owner of your artwork at any given time. Overall, the NFT artwork ecosystem makes it easier for anyone to purchase and sell art.

Creating your NFTs requires little or no technological expertise, contrary to popular belief. You can create NFTs for your artwork in minutes using NFT marketplaces like OpenSea, Rarible, or Mintable.

You must first link your crypto wallet to the NFT marketplace of choice before you can begin building your NFT. You'll never have to share any other information because the wallet address would be your login information. After that, go to the marketplace's "Build" area, upload your artwork and complete the process by pressing the necessary buttons.

That is the end of the discussion. You'll get your NFT artwork ready to sell before your mother summons you downstairs for dinner, your baby begins to weep or your better half misses you.

It is fungible, which means it may be replaced quickly. A one-of-a-kind Mickey Mantle rookie card isn't just any baseball card; it's unique and non-fungible. Because any barrel is as good as the next, oil is fungible.

When non-fungible assets are tokenized, a digital representation of the asset's key data is created. Tokens are kept in wallets, each with its own unique address. Token IDs are linked to wallet addresses on the blockchain, which is a vast, publicly available database that anybody may use to verify digital ownership.

The most common sites for NFT development are OpenSea and Rarible. Although Rarible has the most overall sales, OpenSea offers additional services, such as the ability to build your own NFT website using the OpenSea exchange. Users can upload their artwork and build collections on both platforms without knowing anything about blockchain technology.

Remember that there will be some initial costs before you begin. A blockchain, usually Ethereum's blockchain powers NFTs. To tokenize your art, you'll need to pay a network fee known as gas.

During the development process, Rarible allows artists to mint NFTs on the blockchain (on-chain). As a result, the prices will be lower in the future. Rarible is your best bet if you intend on selling a few NFTs for astronomical prices. You can use OpenSea's Collection Manager, on the other hand, if you want to make a large number of inexpensive NFTs.

Users can create a new set with OpenSea Collection Manager for a one-time fee. The OpenSea centralized team can build and store an infinite amount of NFTs off-chain before a sale is made using that set. Your NFT will be put on the chain and transferred after the buyer pays the transaction's gas tax.

This chapter will guide you through the steps to make your own NFTs in an OpenSea set.

1st Step - Setup MetaMask

Setting up a software wallet is the first step in creating your own NFT. You'll need to use this wallet to store your NFTs and to pay blockchain gas fees.

Go to metamask.io to get the software or install the chrome extension. It is fast and free to create a MetaMask wallet. Only keep hold of your seed phrase in case you need to retrieve the wallet in the future.

Wallets do not hold cryptocurrencies or NFTs; instead, they store your private key, which is required to approve transactions. The blockchain stores both cryptocurrencies and NFTs, and the wallet ID is used to track who owns what.

2ND Step - Tokenize your art

You'll be able to make your NFTs once you've set up a MetaMask wallet. Go to opensea.io and pick Build from the menu bar. You can now use OpenSea to link your MetaMask wallet.

Click the Add New Item button after giving your NFT set a name. Upload the file you want to tokenize and allocate its properties and statistics to set it apart from the rest of your array.

Establish a retail price after determining how many copies of each item you need.

3rd Step - Make a marketplace listing.

You must first authorize OpenSea to sell products from your account before you can sell your first NFT. You would have to pay a gas tax since this is a blockchain purchase. You're good to go if you send any Ether to your MetaMask. This fee is only needed when you create an NFT collection for the first time.

You can buy Ethereum on Coinbase or Gemini and send it to your MetaMask wallet if you don't already have any. Start with Benzinga's guide to buying Ethereum if you're new to cryptocurrencies. Anyone can find and buy NFTs on the OpenSea marketplace now that you've granted OpenSea permission to sell them. It's over!

How to buy NFT

Non-fungible tokens are somewhat distinct from other investments in cryptocurrencies. Like other cryptocurrencies, these tokens do not have value based on their usefulness. Instead, the media attached to NFTs gives them meaning –– the most popular types of media on NFTs today are art and music, but NFTs can tokenize any real-world asset.

NFTs are Ethereum-based tokens that are used to validate ownership of the asset associated with the token. Although NFTs are costly, you are getting more than a JPEG file. Make an account on the NFT Marketplace in the first phase.

NFTs can be bought and sold on various websites. You'll be able to buy various styles of art or collectibles depending on the marketplace you want.

Some of the most well-known NFT marketplaces are as follows:

Opensea is known as an Ethereum-based market for non-fungible tokens. Users can swap non-fungible tokens for cryptocurrencies through the network. It sells everything from video game pieces to digital artwork.

NFTs have their social network called SuperRare. Each piece on the platform is one-of-a-kind and users can purchase and sell these one-of-a-kind pieces through the platform's website. To make a purchase, you'll need to finance your account with Eth tokens since the platform runs on the Ethereum network.

The famous cryptocurrency exchange Gemini owns Nifty Gateway, an NFT marketplace. Famous artists, including Steve Aoki, Grimes, 3LAU, and others, collaborate to release artwork in the primary market.

Collectors may resell their artwork on the company's secondary market. You can use Ethereum to finance your Nifty account or use the website to add a credit card.

NBA Top Shot is a website where you can buy and sell officially licensed NBA memorabilia. These digital basketball cards are more interactive than traditional trading cards and are a new take on basketball cards. In-game clips of the featured teams, for example, are included on the cards.

Step 1

Sorare is an online store where you can buy and sell limited-edition soccer NFT cards. There are currently over 125 clubs listed, with more being added every week. Connect and trade with other fans in Sorare's open marketplace or play the Global Fantasy Football Game, where you can build your lineup and earn points based on real-life results.

Step 2: Deposit into your bank account.

You can buy Ethereum on a cryptocurrency exchange and send your crypto to your marketplace account if you already have an account with one. eToro and Coinbase are decent choices for beginners if you don't have a crypto exchange account already.

Step 3 - Purchase your NFT

Purchasing an NFT is straightforward once your account has been funded. Because most marketplaces are set up as auctions, you'll need to put an offer on the NFT you want to acquire. Some marketplaces work more like an auction for NFTs with a lot of prints, with the highest bid and lowest ask.

The resale value of an NFT purchased straight from the primary market is an added benefit. Shortly after their debut, certain high-demand NFTs will sell for 5 to 10 times their initial price. The drawback of buying NFTs on the open market is that demand is impossible to forecast. You can compare your buy to previous secondary market purchases.

How to sell NFT

Digital trading cards, art, virtual real estate, and gaming are all examples of NFTs. NFTs, unlike common cryptocurrencies such as Bitcoin and Ether, cannot be directly traded and are distributed through some platforms. Most NFT platforms demand that customers have a digital wallet and use cryptocurrencies like Ethereum, WAX, or Flow.

The majority of digital-art trading platforms allow artists to collect royalty. Some art platforms cater to a select group of artists, while others allow everyone to create and sell their work.

NFTs also provided a windfall of benefits for professional digital artists. Last week, Trevor Jones, an NFT artist, told Insider that digital art trading platforms could prevent the need for more traditional art markets.

NFTs have also piqued the interest of many conventional auction houses. Christie's, a 1766-founded auction house, auctioned a Beeple piece in February, marking the company's first foray into the digital token market. With two days left in the auction, the piece is currently valued at $9.75 million.

Platforms like Super Rare, Nifty Gateway Foundation allow buyers to choose from carefully curated work by multimillion-dollar digital artists like Griffin Cock Foster and Beeple. Duncan, co-founders of Nifty Gateway, told Insider that their firm deals with artists one-on-one.

"One of the best things about Nifty Gateway is that there are all these artists who essentially just existed on Instagram or Twitter doing all this very special work but never had a way to make money off it," Griffin Cock told Insider. "They began selling crypto art, and they're still reaping the rewards and gaining popularity."

Names like Grimes and digital comic artist Chris Torres have appeared on Nifty Gateway, Super Rare, and Foundation platforms. Artists will earn up to 10% royalties for all potential sales of their work across these channels.

Although Nifty Gateway aims to make its platform more open to buyers by encouraging them to pay with a credit card, other platforms place a greater emphasis on lowering the entry barrier for developers. Zora and Rarible are invite-only platforms, while Mintable and Rarible allow users to upload and sell images and text as NFTs.

Artists can still receive royalties on these pages, but they aren't as well-curated. Rarible allows users to upload everything from blank pictures to their interpretations of well-known works of art. NFTs can be bought for as little as $10 or as much as hundreds of thousands of dollars on these websites.

OpenSea bills itself as the world's largest non-traditional marketplace, with everything from art to virtual reality, sports, and trading cards available. About 200 categories and 4 million products are available on the website.

On OpenSea, either can be used to purchase common NFT products such as CryptoPunks, CryptoKitties, and virtual real estate. OpenSea has been dubbed "the eBay of the blockchain" by DappRadar, a blog that monitors and analyzes decentralized apps.

Decentraland, a popular virtual real-estate website, is one of the marketplaces that runs on OpenSea. According to DappRadar, OpenSea sold nearly $24 million worth of NFTs in August 2021.

Most expensive NFTs sold

Top 10 Most Expensive NFTs

1. Everydays: the First 5000 Days – $69.3 million

Beeple, the artist, was not as well-known as you might think before last year. He did, however, sell one of the most valuable NFT artworks, "Everydays: the First 5000 Days," on the market in 2021. What made his sale interesting is the fact that it took place at Christie's

The bidding started at a hundred dollars, but it quickly increased, and it was eventually sold for $69.3 million! You could be thinking to yourself, "Wow, that's a lot of money for some digital art." Isn't it evident that, with the technological revolution, we'll soon be moving away from physical paintings and toward digital ones?

2. CryptoPunk #3100 – $7.58 Million

CryptoPunks is a brand-new type of NFT creation and are the first NFTs to hit the market. Many of them are now selling for millions of dollars thanks to the NFT boom! In truth, this CryptoPunk is a one-of-a-kind creature that belongs to a group of nine aliens. CryptoPunks, you see, only has 10,000 punks in stock. Furthermore, only 9 of them are aliens. As you can see, these nine are among their most valuable collections. These tokens are also ERC-20 tokens, which means they adhere to ERC guidelines.

3. CryptoPunk #7804 – $7.57 Million

With $7.57 million, another CryptoPunk in our top ten most expensive NFTs list. Another Alien is the Punk #7804, which comes with three attachments this time. Cap Forward, Small Shades, and a Pipe are among the accessories. Only 254 punks are said to have Cap Forward, 378 punks have Pipe, and 317 punks have little sunglasses. However, the pricing is based on the notion that Alien punks are relatively uncommon.

When the firm originally started giving out the 10,000 CryptoPunks, Dylan Field was the one who got the punk back in. In actuality, he is the founder of the technological design business Figma. But why did he pay so much for that punk? He spotted the potential in this Ethereum-based NFT, which prompted him to purchase it in 2018.

4. Crossroads – $6.6 Million

Crossroads is another another Beeple piece, and it was sold just days before the enormous sale of Everydays. This piece was sold on Nifty Gateway. Crossroads is a single piece of artwork rather and not a compilation. For this reason, the appraisal of this piece makes it even more costly.

On the other side, the artwork posed a political risk. It

was a reaction to the upcoming presidential election in 2020. The artist created two versions of this, one for Trump's election victory and one for his election loss. And the video would alter based on the election results.

5. The first Tweet – $2.9 Million

In truth, after founding Twitter in 2006, CEO and founder Jack Dorsey sent out the first tweet. "Just putting up my twttr," the tweet read. Later, he sold this tweet as an NFT for a whopping $2.9 million! Given the tremendous popularity of the social media site Twitter, it's hardly surprising that the first tweet will receive so much attention. This is a brand-new type of asset tokenization.

In any case, the creator sold this tweet to Oracle CEO Sina Estav, who considers it as significant as purchasing the Mona Lisa. Furthermore, the CEO auctioned off this tweet on Valuables, an online auction platform. They will take a 5% cut from the selling price, according to the platform's terms. Although the tweet will remain on Twitter, Sina is now the owner of the item.

6. CryptoPunk #6965 – $1.54 Million

As previously said, each CryptoPunk has their own own traits and qualities. CryptoPunk #6965, for example, belongs to the Ape family. As an added bonus, it includes a Fedora hat. There are only 186 Fedora-wearing punks, and only 24 Ape-wearing punks. That's why it's $1.54 million. These are ERC-20 coins, not ERC-721 tokens.

7. Axie Infinity Genesis Land – $1.5 Million

If you play virtual games, you are aware of how expensive in-game stuff may be. However, Axie Infinity, an Ethereum-based virtual game, may have pushed it to the next level. Genesis Land is incredibly scarce in the game, and it comes with a significant cost. However, a member of the community recently paid $1.5 million for nine Genesis blocks! As a result, in 2021, it will be one of the most expensive NFTs.

It was valued 888.25 Ether at the time of sale; however, the value has skyrocketed in recent months as the price of Ether has risen as well.

8. CryptoPunk #4156 – $1.25 Million

Next on our list is CryptoPunk #4156, which is the most costly NFT ever sold on the market. That's correct, another CryptoPunk has made it onto our list. This time it's another Ape punk, and this time it comes with a blue bandana as a bonus. Only 481 punks out of a total of 10,000 have this characteristic. For $1.25 million, it now belongs to the Ethereum address 0xf476cd. However, purchasing CryptoPunks will require Ethereum Gas, so keep that in mind if you wish to buy some.

9. Not Forgotten, But Gone – $1 Million

Do you want to spend millions on a gummy bear movie clip that rotates? This is precisely what occurred with the Nifty Gateway NFT sales. WhIsBe is the name of the artist that made this painting. He appears to employ a wide range of gummy bears in a number of creative methods. It's a sixteen-second animation of a golden skeleton bear rotating named "Not Forgotten, But Gone." The artist sold this sculpture for $1 million.

10. Metarift- $904.41K

This is another Satoshi issue, as no one knows who created the artwork. The artist is known as Pak, although no one knows his true identity. Pak is apparently quite popular in the digital art scene, and the piece was sold for $904.41K because of its enigmatic character. Some spherical objects are packed together in the NFT art, and they are rotating in diverse directions. This is only one example of how NFTs can be used; they aren't just for art!

10

HOW TO BECOME A SUCCESSFUL CRYPTOCURRENCY INFLUENCER

"You can be free. You can live and work anywhere in the world. You can be independent from routine and not answer to anybody." - Alexander Elder

Crypto influencer, also known as a Crypto guru, is a person on social media or in the public eye who can affect Cryptocurrency prices or digital coins. Their primary task is to create awareness of digital currencies and blockchain technology while at the same time persuading people to buy and sell digital coins. While influencers use multiple channels, Twitter is one widely used platform as most active conversations occur.

The world of Cryptocurrency continues to grow, and there are certain things to focus on to succeed as a crypto influencer.

Focus on your niche

Your niche, in this case, is Cryptocurrency. The reason you need a specialty is to begin as a miniaturized scale influencer in your specific specialty. Miniaturized scale influencers make an excellent verbal exchange to small gatherings. Small-scale influencers are much less expensive and can achieve a focus on a specialty.

System within the business

To be powerful, you need to make genuine associations. Everybody wants to sit at home on their love seat and interface with influencers via web-based networking media. That is just impossible. Prominent tech influencer iJustine, for instance, has 1.2 million Twitter followers.

Why not make it a priority for promoting yourself? Get off the sofa, get out of the house, and get the chance to real occasions identified with your specialty.

Network

It's insufficient just to react. To become a successful influencer, you need to begin discussions. This kind of commitment is the thing that internet-based life was intended for. And people stay connected on these stages. The more you connect with the community outside of your feed, the further you spread your impact. Don't simply react to remarks on your Facebook page. Post in gatherings, post on companion's pages, and label different influencers to connect with the community. Try not to be reluctant to begin your very own Facebook gathering to attract much more adherents.

Tune in to criticism

Being a maker of any sort or in the open eye in any capacity whatsoever includes handling a great deal of criticism. Indeed, even the President of the United States or the most extravagant man on the planet can't keep away from criticism. No measure of cash or power can!

However, so few of us can handle it. If you become an individual who can handle helpful criticism, critics will shape you into a more cleaned influencer. Being an influencer isn't tied in with directing what people do. It's tied in with making development, and useful criticism is fundamental to that. No one wants to be encompassed by yes men.

Platforms for your channels

As a Cryptocurrency influencer, you will work on different platforms, including Youtube, Instagram, and Clubhouse.

Teens can earn extra money by advertising their gigs on Fiver etc., by doing a shout out, shilling, and promote new crypto, nft, or any token on Twitter or any social media channel. As mentioned earlier, Twitter is a widely used platform by crypto influencers.

Telegram

Telegram has recently found a home with cryptocurrency developers, traders, and entrepreneurs. You might wonder what has made Telegram an attractive platform for traders and investors. I will discuss a few aspects that have pushed telegram to blockchain stardom.

Privacy

Telegram is popular because it is more private than its well-known competitors. The contents of personal communications are not accessible to governments, regulators, or other bodies in this circumstance. To enjoy complete anonymity, some users choose to utilize Telegram's stop-to-stop encryption feature. Given the uncertain criminal climate in which cryptocurrencies exist, privacy may be essential if one buys and sells interests that may attract notice.

Telegram has become well-known in sections of the sector that are authoritarian or repressive. Governments may also choose to stymie the operations of popular messaging apps by blocking access via cellular or fixed-line networks. In these places, buyers may turn to Telegram in order to avoid government crackdowns that could otherwise disrupt communications.

News channels

Since Telegram now supports every automated bot and RSS service, some bitcoin investors, news websites, and other media have formed broadcast groups that might provide information to Telegram users in an unexpected way.

At the same time, Telegram Channels can handle a limitless number of users, as Telegram supergroups can hold up to 100,000 members at once. In bitcoin circles, as Telegram Channels permits brands to send messages and updates to their legitimate potential – using their name rather than that of a regular customer – makes brand-building an effective workout.

Price bots

Telegram has stayed committed to developing bot services on its platform, unlike several other messaging systems. Interested developers can use telegram's API and documentation and third-party libraries to build bots.

Several traders have used this capability to build price bots that automatically inject real-time price updates into their chats. Telegram users have constructed bots that can provide price updates at major milestones or margins, or have utilized bots to stay informed of arbitrage opportunities on several exchanges, in addition to supplying relevant price information in numerous cryptocurrencies.

An impending ICO

Telegram is now conducting the world's largest initial coin offering (ICO).Telegram wants to launch a personal blockchain platform called "Telegram Open Community (TON)" soon. The platform would launch with the promise of allowing citizens of repressive nations to send money via the app, with the platform's foreign money being referred to as the 'Gram.'

Telegram is said to have raised USD 1.7 billion in a

private pre-sale, and it's unclear whether the service will have a public crowdsale anytime soon.

Twitter

Social media is a popularity contest. These days, everyone is on Twitter, including your friends and family, favorite celebrities, and favorite brand. Cryptocurrency influencers use Twitter widely to spread news, evangelize, shindle coins, or shame other crypto projects. The more followers you have, the greater the influence.

So if you want to get followers fast and increase your followers fast, try these suggestions:

Promote your presence on Twitter in all of your assets, including print media (such as a Follow Us on Twitter message with Twitter icon) and digital media. If people don't know that you are on Twitter, they can't follow you there. Include your Twitter handle wherever you can, including on business cards, physical printed flyers, magazine or newspaper ads, etc. For digital media, do the same but ensure the media is hyperlinked to your Twitter channel so that readers can simply click and access.

Tweet frequently. If you have the resources to do so, you should be tweeting anywhere from one to 30 times per day, as long as the content is relevant and engaging.

Timeliness is critical for Twitter, as there are 500 million tweets sent per day. However, the challenge with Twitter is that it tends to highlight activity out of order based on the interests of its followers. So, posting at off-peak hours could cause you to miss out on a significant amount of engagement.

The Scoop with the Hashtag

If you're unclear on what hashtags are, hashtags leverage keywords or phrases that are placed together without spaces and then are preferred with that # symbol. In most cases, they are used to reference events, key goings-on in the entertainment industry, or recurring themes.

The development of your hashtag strategy is critical to creating engagement with your followers. In fact, it is believed that the use of a hashtag will increase engagement by more than 10%. Effective use of a hashtag can and will help you to increase your followers.

Every tweet can use as many hashtags as you want, but Twitter recommends no more than two hashtags per tweet.

Also, check what hashtags your influencers (or ideal influencers) are using. Since these people are spokespersons for various industries, they are viewed as experts in the space and perform well on social media, partially due to how and what hashtags they use to draw in more and more followers.

The 10 Most Popular Hashtags on Twitter

According to Hubspot, these are the 25 best hashtags to get likes on a tweet: I will mention the top ten in this chapter;

Ico

Ethereum

Crypto

Crowdfunding

Medicaid

Blackhistorymonth

Womenshistorymonth

Photography

iwd2018

Cryptocurrency

YouTube

Video-sharing is perhaps one of the most influential tactics to use in digital marketing. As human beings, we are visual creatures, regarding visual stimulation being more pleasurable and memorable than written text or shared images. A video is also a powerful tool for storytelling; we can explain concepts more efficiently, give believable product reviews, and share our unique personalities with others. Over the years, there has been a rise in video-sharing due to increased access to the Internet, smarter technological devices, and improved internet connections.

YouTube is by far the most popular video-sharing platform globally, boasting 2 billion registered users worldwide. This platform is a popular choice for video streaming among the young and the old alike. Businesses have joined the YouTube community, with nearly 8 out of 10 (78.8%) marketers considering the platform an effective marketing tool (Mohsin, 2020). YouTube has the power to increase a company's visibility among its video-loving target audience. It provides opportunities for companies, such as car manufacturers or beauty brands, to easily share their current news and product updates and receive feedback from their customers through YouTube comments.

Although many other social media platforms allow users to upload and share videos easily, many brands still prefer to share extended and more in-depth videos on social media channels like YouTube. I am yet to find another platform that gives brands the ability to demonstrate the use or function or capture an individual's personality in such detail in an edited and content-rich YouTube video. Therefore, I find that YouTube is a great video-sharing platform, useful in sharing experiences and content that prompts engagement from the targeted audience.

As a Crypto Influencer, you can build your brand on YouTube by creating relatable video content that would allow viewers to buy into the brand and learn more about the influencer's value offer. The best way to gain a following on YouTube is to decide on a particular niche, in this case, cryptocurrency, which you hope to dominate. After, take some time to view other people's channels who have already created a name for themselves in that specific niche. After conducting your research, you will see a gap within your niche that isn't occupied yet. This notable gap will become your unique value proposition, which you will leverage to build your brand. From then onwards, your task will be to create engaging content that explores various themes and topics related to your particular value offer.

Instagram

The concept of "influencer marketing" began on Instagram when the popular social media platform introduced us to visual storytelling. This app, which is now worth over $100 billion, offered creatives and brands a space to maximize the use of images to connect with like-minded people. Perhaps Instagram is favored by influencers more than other social networking sites because it is easy to find and create communities on the platform, resulting in a curated experience instead of being cluttered with irrelevant content. One of the reasons most influencers will have an Instagram account (among their list of other social media accounts) is that Instagram reigns supreme when it comes to engagement.

Indeed, Instagram makes building a personal brand a breeze because there are multiple ways of creating meaningful content. Connecting to your target audience is achievable through the use of targeted hashtags and posts. It is also easier to differentiate your brand on Instagram by using unique themes, filters, photography, and quirky content ideas. Instagram is also useful for influencer marketing because it is one of the few social media platforms that have created a lucrative environment for brand ambassadorship. It is common for users to see one of their friends promoting a new product from a local business or recommending the services because brands love to use Instagram for authentic product reviews, campaigns, and new releases. This is because a picture can tell a thousand words, especially when shared within closed communities.

Influencer marketing on Instagram is effective because an advertisement doesn't feel or look like one. Rather, the content can take on any tone, style, or message, depending on the influencer endorsing it and its caption. What would've sounded corny using traditional advertising is pulling at the heartstrings of the target audience and evoking a passion, longing, or desire for the product or service. Therefore, I would say that Instagram's superpower lies in creating imagery to relate, connect, and empathize with the target audience. Influencers also can build relationships with their followers, strengthening their promotional activities and sponsored campaigns. By the time brands approach them for work opportunities, the influencers have built a loyal community of followers willing to listen, engage, and act on the influencer's leadership and instruction.

Many people debate over what exactly qualifies an individual to become an Instagram influencer. While you may find many different standards or criteria online regarding this controversial topic, I will share my thoughts on how you will know once you have "made it" on Instagram. Firstly, let me start by saying the number of followers does not determine an influencer. Nowadays, followers may be ghost followers (fake bot profiles), or followers are often bought. The problem with buying followers is that they do not necessarily fit into the target audience you want to promote to—and this won't help brands when they come knocking at your door either.

The level of engagement that an individual can create on

their Instagram page qualifies them as an influencer. I say this because the only proof brands have of the influencer having some social media power is if their followers are physically engaging through comments and following the influencer's instructions. In essence, brands are looking for influencers who have firm control over their brand and can manage and influence their community to buy a product or view a website through clever content and messaging.

The Effectiveness of Using Mixed Media

I have often heard people say, "If you didn't Instagram it, it didn't happen." It is sentiments like these that show the popularity and power of Instagram in creating and sharing valuable content. Perhaps another element provided by Instagram that allows brands to produce interesting content easily is the many ways content can be created on the platform. Most social media platforms host content but fail to provide an in-house content-generating machine similar to what we find on Instagram. The ability to constantly alternate the type of content you share as an influencer keeps your followers hungry for more. Therefore, playing around with various media and content will help you communicate the same message about your brand in many ways. Below are some of the unique types of content that you can create using Instagram:

Instagram Stories

Instagram stories are a great tool to use when you have interesting daily content to share with your community, which may not necessarily be appropriate for the theme or campaign that you are promoting on your feed. Instagram stories can also be used in campaigns or collaborations to share clickable links to websites or other Instagram pages. You must represent your brand in your stories because stories can draw new visitors visiting your page for the first time. View your Instagram stories as your daily or weekly sales pitch to explain why your brand is unique and valuable. You can heighten your stories' visual appeal by adding music, moving graphics, behind-the-scenes videos, and quirky descriptions.

Carousel Ads

Carousel ads were first developed on Facebook's platform; however, they have become a major hit on Instagram. To simply put it, a carousel ad is a form of advertisement that allows the promoter to include a variety of images and videos into one ad format. Usually, carousel ads can show three to five images or videos in one ad unit, giving the promoter plenty of room to sell their value proposition. Influencers, in particular, can use carousel ads to tell a story about the brand that they are promoting (this can also include your brand). You can tell a story about a product's various features or benefits or show unique aspects of your brand that will encourage Instagram users to visit your page.

IGTV

IGTV and Instagram are two separate downloadable apps (similar to Facebook Messenger and Facebook); however, they work together to uplift the quality of influencers' content. The main purpose of IGTV is to allow users to create and share videos that are perhaps too long to post on an Instagram story (however, unlike Instagram story videos, these long-form videos can stay on your channel permanently). Influencers can use IGTV to produce shareable video content on Instagram while also including meaningful "Swipe Up" call-to-actions on their video content. Some of the content you can share through IGTV are tutorials for using products, discussing a topic or answering community questions, documenting your day, or producing your own Instagram show or series. Once you have created your IGTV video, you can always cross-promote it by sharing a link to your video on your Instagram story.

Instagram Live Videos

Instagram live videos are gaining more popularity now than ever before. The advantage of using Instagram live videos is that your video content can stream in real-time. Moreover, they provide a great opportunity for influencers and brands to communicate directly to their fans in real-time. I would encourage the use of live videos once your Instagram page has shown signs of positive engagement. In cases like this, regular live videos can boost the traffic that comes onto your page and increase your community's number of loyal followers. Some of the content that you can share on an Instagram live video is behind-the-scenes footage in real-time. This may include footage taken at an event or festival that you are attending. Your live video can also show a tour around your office or home, cooking recipes in real-time, and taking the time to be transparent with your followers, sharing personal stories, or discussing a trend.

Instagram Reels

Instagram's latest add-on has a striking resemblance to TikTok. Instagram Reels are the platform's newest offering, allowing users an opportunity to record 15-second clips with Instagram's selection of music added onto them. This feature creates yet another form of media on the platform, helping content creators create fun and engaging short clips. These clips reflect on the Explore page, Instagram Stories and appear on the new Reels tab on user profiles. Users can scroll through short clips from their friends and popular or trending Instagram accounts on the Reels feed. When a Reel appears on the Explore page, Instagram will notify the user and add a "Featured" tag on the bottom left corner of their video. While the Reels algorithm remains unknown at this point, the criteria of making your Reels featured is likely dependent on the originality and entertainment value of the Reels. While IGTV delivers on series-based full-length content, Reels provide high-quality informal content with a shelf life longer than twenty-four hours.

What is Crypto Shilling?

A "shill" or "Shiller" is someone who actively encourages people to invest in cryptocurrencies. The price and interest in the coin or token rise as they market it, tempting people to buy.

A Shiller is nearly always a scammer in the crypto world. They could have bought cryptocurrencies intending to resell them for a profit. In addition, numerous cryptocurrency projects provide incentives to influencers who "shill" the project.

The term "shill" does not originate in the crypto world. Casinos all across the world, for example, use shills regularly. The collaborators are given a stack of chips to play with to ensure that the other gamblers are not alone in their losses.

What defines a shill is a question of your preference. We can see shilling when someone makes unfavorable, often false, accusations.

John McAfee and Elon Musk

Like many other crypto influencers, John McAfee used his celebrity to endorse crypto startups and tokens during the 2017 ICO boom. He admits to charging $105,000 per tweet and promoting a coin by allegedly taking a significant portion of the overall supply.

Others act as advocates for cryptocurrency in general,

while some promote projects with a stake. Some Bitcoin influencers include Saifedean Ammous (author of The Bitcoin Standard), the Winklevoss twins (founders of cryptocurrency exchange Gemini), MicroStrategy CEO Michael Saylor, and Tesla CEO Elon Musk, defend crypto against its naysayers.

Musk's name is always referenced when Bitcoin influencers are mentioned. As a result of the tech billionaire's tweets, the Bitcoin (and Dogecoin) markets have moved. Hundreds of thousands of comments and millions of interactions resulted.

Clubhouse

The clubhouse is an audio-only app that allows anyone on the app to host a room to talk about literally anything they want to.

As users get on Clubhouse and use the app more and more, it's developing its own culture and its own etiquette. There have been many hosted rooms on it that have attempted to address the question of what exactly Clubhouse is, so this isn't a totally easy and clear-cut question to answer, but I'll do my best.

Think of it this way, imagine going to a dinner party with a few friends you know, but you inevitably meet new people at that party, and the cool thing about dinner parties is they don't typically have a closing time.

How many times have you gone to a friend's house and stood at the door to leave but ended up staying another hour just talking? It's hard to leave great conversations, and there have been rooms that have run perpetually for incredibly long periods.

For example, On December 27th, 2020, a room was started in the "We Drop Gems Club," That room stayed open until January 8, 2021, a record-breaking 12 days and 38 minutes straight...

And how do rooms stay open for so long, you ask? Are people talking for 12 days straight? Well, yes and no. You see, think of the larger Clubhouse rooms like an auditorium. You have the audience and the stage. You might have two people on stage talking, or you might have 52 people on stage speaking.

Audience members can also speak if they raise their hand and are selected from the moderators to join the conversation. So naturally, you have people coming and going from the stage and coming and going from the audience. Some people are leaving the auditorium, and some people are coming into it and joining.

After all, as the saying goes, - it's five o'clock somewhere, and being a global app makes this type of 24/7 conversation an actual reality. Further than that, it's incredibly addicting, and some people are spending all their free hours every week on Clubhouse. Many people even use it as a radio replacement while working, just passively listening to the conversations. There are many ways to use and participate in the app, and because of this, a room can theoretically run in perpetuity and never end.

So, it's like a house party that simply just *never ends*. That's kind of insane to think about, but it's true, and the Clubhouse app makes it all possible!

AFTERWORD

Thank you for reading this book!

In this book, you were introduced to all the different concepts you need to understand before stepping into the world of cryptocurrencies. Learning about cryptos takes considerable time and effort. However, now that you are armed with the fundamentals of investing in cryptos and the risks involved, it is time to get started. By now, you probably realize investing in cryptos and understanding the blockchain network isn't as intimidating as you probably thought.

Be open to learning, hone your basic understanding of cryptos, practice different trading strategies, and start investing in this market!

Good Luck,

Alexander Knight

BOOK DESCRIPTION

Do you know Cryptocurrencies have become one of the most prevalent investment opportunities for the world in 2021? Are you interested to learn how to invest in cryptocurrency and build a wealthy dream future for tomorrow? If yes, then keep reading!

As a beginner, you might feel doubtful and hesitant at first. You might think that it is a scam or that it has no real value. A lot of people think and feel this way. Some believe that many countries will not recognize cryptocurrency trading, so there is no point in making investments. Others feel that cryptocurrency trading is merely a fad that will fade out in just a few years.

However, these negative assumptions are incorrect. The biggest economies in the world recognize Bitcoin as an official currency. India, Japan, and the United States are only some major countries that consider cryptocurrency an asset.

Being a teenager is among the best times to invest since you possess certain luxuries that you don't have as an adult. You have virtually no expenses and have all the time on your side. You have the unique ability to create an investment portfolio and build wealth entirely uninterrupted by the bills and costs of everyday life.

Investing in cryptocurrency is an excellent way you can grow your money. Although relatively new on the market, it is legit. Once you understand how it works, you will be confident to trade it. Today, you will find a variety of platforms that help individuals start cryptocurrency trading.

This book is intended to prepare you to succeed in cryptocurrency investing, with the encompassing mission being to ensure the financial freedom of its readers. Most people aren't exposed to this information at your age, so be careful with it. Please treat it with care and understand its importance. Most importantly, use it. It's truly powerful and can change your life if you put in the time and the work.

Here is what you will learn!

- Ways you can earn money as a teenager to invest in cryptocurrency
- How to buy and invest in bitcoin
- Bitcoin and blockchain
- How to make money on meme coins
- NFTs and how to create them
- Some of the most expensive NFTs ever sold
- How to protect yourself from scammers
- Initial Coin Offering (ICOs)
- How to become a cryptocurrency influencer

And much more. Tap into the wealth creation potential the crypto market is offering you right now.

Printed in Great Britain
by Amazon